A MEMOIR

# Coach Life

## *How Wanderlust Turned a Bored Baby Boomer into a Happy Camper*

Alexis Hartz

**Simply Living Publications**
**Bayfield, CO 81122**

For information about special discounts for bulk purchase please contact the publisher at 877-236-0938 or info@AlexisHartz.com

Cover Art: Adreana Marie Cerda
Editor: Sara Lynn Valentine
Book Layout © 2014 BookDesignTemplates.com

**Coach Life / Alexis Hartz**. -- 1st ed.

Library of Congress Control Numbers:
2016907689

ISBN 978-0-9974497-0-9 (pbk)
ISBN 978-0-9974497-1-6 (ebook)

# CONTENTS

# { 1 }

# Prologue

Some people live their dreams on purpose. Not me. I trip into them by default. Except this one. It was different.

I'd held it in the back of my mind for years and never expected it to materialize. However, the more I witnessed death impetuously swipe unsuspecting mortals off the planet, the more I realized how limited my time was. So I *decided* to push this dream into existence.

Without a plan or an ounce of regret I became a workcamper, a gypsy of sorts, who makes a living out of a home on wheels. I bought a motor home, buckled myself into the driver's seat and took off with a tankful of blissful optimism.

Some pitied me. Others questioned my sanity. Dear friends knew that I began living a dream that took decades to materialize. They were awestruck. But I was challenged from the start.

I didn't know diddly-squat about RVs when I purchased mine. The day I picked it up from the previous owner I got a short and sweet tutorial on the basic mechanical functions after which he announced, "Now the fun part. Time to 'load' the car!"

He's referring to positioning my passenger car on the one-axle tow dolly that I'll pull behind my ginormous new home on wheels. I feel palpably incompetent.

Cautiously anticipating the "fun part" I settle into my sage green Saturn sedan and grasp the steering wheel. With a hesitant toe on the gas pedal, and guided by my patient instructor, I gingerly nudge the wheels up the narrow tow trailer ramps. I feel the car's weight level the ramps. I drop the gearshift into neutral and . . . KA-boom! Instead of cradling into a comfortable traveling position one of the front tires land on the ramp's sharp iron lip and explodes.

My instructor assesses the damage and assures me that the tire must be repaired prior to hauling the car anywhere. So I reverse directions and tap the gas pedal again. As I back the car down the tire ramps I hear a click!-click!-click!-click!-click! and see that one by one the clips that secure the bumper to the car's front end are catching on the trailer's center toggle bolt, tearing the bumper right off the car. I stop mid-ramp and cringe at the damage. I feel like I'm ripping a scab off a skinned knee.

But my mentor coaches me onward, "Keep going! It'll be okay."

I do as I'm told, unload my cute car with a flat tire and a drooping bumper. Buyer's remorse oppresses me as I toddle around the mutilated vehicle.

"No worries, I can fix all of this," he assures me. He pops in and out of his garage with clips for the bumper and an air jack for the tire. As promised he mounts the spare tire and puts the bumper back where it belongs. The repairs don't take long but the delay means that now I'll be driving smack dab through Phoenix in rush hour traffic. This is not what I planned and definitely not how I expected my dream to feel.

My three-hour trip home is grueling. My fists clench the steering wheel. My muscles are tense from my eyeballs to my buttocks. Sweat drips from every pore on my body. I am imprisoned with condemning thoughts that perhaps I have just made the very worst decision of my life. I constantly check my mirrors, pleased that *most* of the time I am only driving in one lane.

Still gripped with fear and now exhausted too, I park in front of my suburban home. End to end as long as the lot the house stands on, and high enough to block the view of the two-story home across the street, my secret purchase is now fully exposed. I am "outed" like a closeted gay girl with a stylish haircut and penchant for men's clothing. With the truth in plain view I struggle to rest in the fulfillment of my dream.

I turn off the ignition and let out a deep sigh. I stretch my spider legs out from under the steering wheel, sling them over the center console and clumsily plant each foot in the "living room". I take two short steps, plop down on the couch and entertain rambling thoughts of abounding landscapes that I will soon travel through. . .

I leave my daydreams, stand up and walk two steps into the compact kitchen to survey the space. I quickly map out where a coffee maker, a tin of cooking utensils, my copper cookware, a Dutch oven and a mixing bowl will fit. I have room for everything I need to create epicurean delights in my travel-size kitchenette.

I take two more steps, turn, open the closet doors next to the kitchen table and assess the itsy-bitsy clothing storage space. Then I tread through the short hallway between the shower and the bathroom to my new bedroom. Visions of snuggling into fluffy featherbedding between clean, white flannel sheets lure me into relaxation . . .

It's been four years since I crossed the threshold of my formidable RV. What follows in these pages is an account of why this journey began, how I lived through the first twelve months and what I learned along the way.

My sun-burned decade-old rig screams white trash on the outside, but inside it is a haven of peaceful delights and unexpected possibilities. Minimalism is my new opulence and transitory neighbors like the Paul Bunyan Texan out-perform reality TV characters every day of the week.

Every inch of this home feels more like home that every foot of every other place I have lived. And why shouldn't it? It is my very own real life dream machine.

# { 2 }

# Fueled by Regret

I spent the year before I bought my RV with my self-sustaining and stubbornly independent mother, Genevieve, in her home in Michigan. It was the last year of her life. I watched her die of cancer.

Well, that's not exactly true. I mean, yes, she did have cancer, and yes, that probably would have eventually killed her. But cancer wasn't the only thing gnawing away at her otherwise healthy body. Experimental drugs and their desultory side effects took their toll on her quality of life. I was her untrained personal assistant and N-RN (non-registered nurse). With only on-the-job training I fumbled to keep her fed, clothed, clean, comfortable and properly medicated.

I watched her systematically exit her life. She cleaned out and donated the contents of her closets and drawers. She researched funeral homes and memorial services and ways to dispose of her body. She designated responsibilities to her four children, each with their own lives in states across the country. One of my brothers was in charge of overseeing the finances and executing her will. My other brother was charged with managing the upkeep of her home and preparing it for market after she died. My sister, the youngest, was to fill in wherever necessary, mostly with visits to relieve me of my duties for a few days at a time.

We arranged our schedules around her dwindling energy supply. But friends and relatives wanting to see Genevieve one last time arrived and stayed at their leisure, unaware of how taxing their visits were on her. Always hospitable Genevieve would entertain them as if cancer was conveniently taking time off. She'd switch her focus from preparing for death to preparing for her guests as if they were the ones needing a break from reality.

One week after her 70th birthday the visiting hospice nurse advised me that Genevieve's passing was imminent. My brothers and sister booked flights to Michigan immediately after my call to each of them. Late in the evening of their arrival we sat at her bedside posed like models for a Norman Rockwell portrait. We sat still and quiet, waiting for her to take her last breath. An hour passed. Then another. We expected something to happen. She rested peacefully. So we left her bedside to unpack and settle in for the wait.

Hours turned into days. As our mother wrestled with the dying process we wrestled with where we all would sleep and how to fill our days. We decided to begin some of the tasks on Genevieve's postmortem To-Do list. First on the list: the family photo collection.

We set up her old slide projector and projection screen and opened the first of three briefcases full of slides. Lounged on the couch, stretched out on over-sized pillows on the white carpeted floor, and with feet up on easy chairs we turned her proper living room into a home theater. There, a floor below where Genevieve lay semi-conscious between two worlds we revisited our youth.

We reminisced over images of our family at the beach, camping in the mountains, and trips to off-the-beaten-path destinations. We shared memories of times spent with each other and with extended family. We were stunned at how different our perspectives were about our shared experiences. We laughed at each other. And we cried together. And we mocked our family's inclination to dress in plaid, all of us, in varying colors and checked dimensions in slide after slide.

Once the slides were viewed and divvied up we started on the furniture. Quietly and systematically we addressed each item in every room. Then we dealt with funeral arrangements. We planned a Celebration of Life ceremony, hired a caterer and made a guest list. Was it dishonorable to take care of what needed to be done eventually while she was still living? We wrestled with that too, but we knew that we were making the best use of this waiting time. And we knew that Genevieve would approve.

For those last two weeks the four of us and two spouses were sequestered in her home. We played tens of hours of Mexican Dominoes together, watched our favorite family movies and over-indulged in overly caloric classic comfort foods. Bloody Marys became our breakfast beverage of choice. We hadn't spent that much time together since we left her home as young adults.

With each passing day we wondered if hearing our voices and laughter galvanized Genevieve to cling to her dear life. We completed the postmortem To-do list, and with nothing else to do but continue over-eating and over-drinking we decided to test our theory. All but I left her home one evening to return to their own homes. The following morning Genevieve passed from this world to the next. I suppose that once she knew the party was over she gave in to death's inevitable arrival.

That year I learned the value of time and the silliness of stuff. Genevieve had lived a full and comfortable life. She had poured hours of time into hobbies and volunteer activities and visits with friends. She lived in a professionally decorated home set on a professionally land-scaped lot. She traveled regularly and had a fully-funded retirement. Her life was charmed not by excess inherited wealth, but rather by her innate and keenly practical financial wizardry. She struggled with times of scarcity but in the end she surrounded herself with only the things and people that brought her joy.

The only thing she took with her was her regrets. She had many of them. I'll never forget the days when Genevieve tearfully confessed her regrets to me. She hadn't trusted her own abilities enough. She hadn't set large enough goals for herself. She hadn't forgiven enough. And she hadn't been transparent enough in the relationships she cherished the most.

Her regrets and confessions haunted me. Their acidic pain leached into my conscience forcing me to consider what regrets I might have about my own life. I realized then that there was only one way to avoid such bitter pain. I had to acknowledge my possible regrets and imme-diately take action. I had to start making decisions accordingly.

After Genevieve's death I moved back to my beautiful home in Ari-zona, the home that I had furnished, decorated, and cared for in hopes of luring my "boyfriend" (a workaholic 50-year-old bachelor) of six years into sharing a life with me. But like most well-meaning providers his corporate commitment came first, and that didn't change just be-cause I had. I spent nearly a year trying to imprint my new perspective on him but he remained committed to collecting things and funds for the life of his dreams. Time together was an occasional extravagance. The big payoff would come with retirement, with both time and things in abundance.

I veered in the opposite direction. Without any responsibilities, ob-ligations, or a job, I was free to snatch up my dream life immediately. For years I had told friends and co-workers that all I wanted to do was live in an RV and travel the country and help people. Up to now it had been a fantasy. I hadn't consciously expected it ever to be real. But now I felt like my only option was to make it happen or go to my grave regretting that I didn't.

I kept my plan a secret as I took action towards its fruition. I didn't want to be discouraged by naysayers and realists. The palpable power of potential regret continually fueled me. It overrode the safety of a permanent home and the security of fully-funded retirement.

I searched and planned. I thought about where I would go, whether I would tow my car behind an RV or tow a camper behind a new super-powered pickup truck. I evaluated how much space I wanted and compared that to how much I needed. I looked through the classified ads for used RVs. I visited sales lots and talked over my choices with dealers and owners. I slimmed down my possessions and prepared myself for teeny-tiny RV living. I employed the same processes that my mother did as she shut down her past life and prepared for her entry into heaven. My heaven would be here on earth, complete with four wheels and a good strong engine.

I was terrified to tell anyone, especially my grown sons. I waited until a motor home was titled in my name before I emailed an announcement to my family.

Both sons replied with enthusiastic thumbs up. Pursuing my dream was giving them permission and confidence to pursue their own – confirmation that I was on the right track.

# { 3 }

# Announcement

*I'm sharing this email with you knowing that we agree on this:*

*We all want our children to be happy.*
*We want them to have fulfilling lives, to be free of want, fear, injury and regret.*
*We want to encourage them in every way possible to pursue and live their dreams.*

*It's been my lifelong dream to live in an RV and gad about the country and help people.*
*As Pollyanna-ish as that sounds, I know that God has much more in store for me on this journey than what I can express in my simple-minded dream.*
*In fact, I am so sure that I've taken the necessary actions to live it.*

*I have purchased a 32' motor home and the necessary equipment to tow my car with me.*

*As people who love and care about me, you're probably asking a question or two right now.*

*Some of you want to know about the vehicle and project logistics.*
*Some of you are wondering about my security and safety.*
*Some of you are searching the web for mental health resources which you may include in your reply to me.*

*I hope that some of you are so excited for me that you realized that I can't not do this.*

*Believe me, I've had every thought that you're having and answered every question*
*with multiple answers already*
*– more than just a few times during the many months of evaluating this venture.*

*So, knowing you all love and care about me*
*I ask that no matter what, you wish me well.*

*Remember that I am smart and logical.*
*I know how to take care of myself.*
*I can figure things out.*
*I am a problem solver.*
*I am not perfect and when I make mistakes*
*I'll learn and know more for the future.*

*As people who love and care about me,*
*pray for me . . . daily . . . please.*

*As people who love and care for me,*
*please read my blog.*
*Post replies. Send emails. Call. Write.*
*I want and will need your encouragement.*

*I want to share the goodness of the days with you.*

*Love, Alexis*

# { 4 }

# Workcamper

Now that the RV is parked on the street in front of my home I know it won't be long before the HOA police will be issuing a citation. So I give it a thorough cleaning and drive it to the Big Toys Storage Lot. Out of sight but not out of mind.

My next step is to figure out where I will go and how I will support myself. I have no idea how to do that without a permanent address. I'm not a ladder-climbing corporate executive with a field of expertise or a pension. I do however, have a wealth of professional experiences to draw upon and I've excelled at every position I've held.

My resume reads like help wanted ads, plenty of variety and pay rates, but not an inkling of continuity. I have experience in retail and wholesale, administration, registration, observation and training. I've held management positions and sales positions, and always had some sort of entrepreneurial venture going on the side.

I know the professional way to clean a house. I can cook a meal for 20 and execute a party for hundreds. I can design a garden, lay sod, split firewood and sculpt rose bushes. I can paint a room, a house, and a portrait. I can hem a skirt and tailor a suit. I can care for kids, pets and grandparents. I know how to balance a checkbook, live within a budget and work hard to get what I want. Surely one of these skills will keep food in my belly and gas in my tank on the road.

I turn to the internet and start searching with great apprehension. But with a few clicks of my mouse I am transported into a world that has been waiting for me my entire life! The fear of finding my calling on the road morphs into finally finding my calling when I learn that I am a workcamper in the most accomplished sense of the word.

Workcamper. That's what those of us who live in RVs are called by the employers who hire us. You'd think finding steady employment would be challenging for a transient nomad but quite the opposite is true. Websites galore court those of us who are free to come and go as we please to any place we choose.

I find positions available in cities, on beaches, in the mountains, in this country and in other countries. I can work in amusement parks, national parks, or in RV parks. Employers advertise part-time positions, full-time positions, and make-your-own schedule positions. Required skill sets vary from being able to pick up trash to reading topographical maps to inspect gas drilling sites. There are jobs for young and old. There are high-paying positions and volunteer positions and all rates of pay in between.

I'm overwhelmed with the choices and thrilled that my Millennial tendency to job-hop is now an advantage rather than an objection to overcome. I sketch out a geographical plan to my liking then hunker down at my desk and begin submitting resumes to prospective employers. I apply for a position with BuyItOnline.com for the holiday season. Next I apply for a spring gig during the Major League Baseball training season in Tempe, Arizona. Hopefully I'll secure a position at Mesa

Verde National Park in Colorado for the summer. If I don't get the positions, I know where to find plenty more that suit my fancy.

Now with potential employers identified and my initial travel schedule outlined I claim my new professional title: Workcamper.

# { 5 }

# Stuff

The workcamper job search has led me to a treasure trove of valuable information about RV living, including how to evaluate what to take with me on the road. It's all about weight. It's easy to exceed the manufacturer's recommended weight allowance and overload a vehicle. I must carefully consider how much each of my precious belongings (PB's) weighs and take only what I need.

I'm in the final stages of preparing for departure. The movers come tomorrow. All of my PBs except those needed in the motor home will be boxed up and stored until I unpack them in my retirement home. If this dream journey is as fulfilling as I expect it to be these PBs could be resting in storage for a decade or more.

A few weeks ago I inventoried my PBs and send the list to my sons thinking they might want one or two of them in their own homes. I also showed the list to friends and asked them if they needed or wanted any of my PBs. Sad to say, most of what I offered was rejected. Tough to handle and admit, but better to know now than ten years from now with thousands of dollars invested in storing the unwanted junk.

Today while I pack my PBs I think about how much they have already influenced the course of my life. I've kept high-paying, stressful jobs so that I could buy this cool stuff and give other cool stuff to my sons. I now have a houseful of PBs that none of us – I, nor my boyfriend, nor my sons appreciate. And Genevieve has shown me that much of it will get tossed when I die anyway!

After hauling a big donation to the local thrift store I place the precious few remaining PBs into storage boxes with thoughtful eulogies. I reminisce over where each came from, how much I love and will miss each. And then I consider again . . .one more time . . . if I will need any of them on my journey.

Will I need it? Instantly my heart rate increases and my palms start to sweat. Will I need it? I wonder again. If I do, how will I get it? What will I do without it?

I quickly halt my senseless fear and panic. I remind myself that I live in a consumer-driven culture. I'm conditioned to want more than I need.

I pause, take a deep breath and calm myself. I remember that I have only 300 square feet of living space available. I can live without what I am leaving behind. And if I can't, I can pick up a replacement at the local superstore any time.

I refocus and continue to pack. It's the journey, not the stuff that's important.

# { 6 }

# Cat

I'll have a roommate for this adventure. She's my cat. I call her Cat. No sense in giving her some cute name. She won't respond to it anyway. That's just the way cats are. Not their most endearing quality, but they find ways to make up for it.

I was raised in a dog-loving household. Cats were considered out-door rodent controllers, not pets. I never considered owning one myself, especially before I married my European husband. But after spending a few short weeks with him and his over-sized, long-haired, spoiled-rotten, pure-white cat named Rambo I became a cat lover myself.

After we divorced I decided to adopt a feline of my own. Princess, an eight-year-old tortoise-shell reclusive female fell short of my expectations after my experience with Rambo. She never warmed up to me and rarely acknowledged any of my affections toward her. But I still loved her. Shortly after she arrived my sons gifted me with Junior, an identically colored kitten from their barn cat's litter. I was on my way to being a Cat Lady before I even knew their reputation as romance-challenged spinsters.

Not long after acquiring my second feline I met and married a con man. (So much for being a romance-challenged spinster.) Marriage to the con man came with a price, a rather large one. In order to have a life with him he insisted that I give up my cats. (Clearly this was just one of the red flags in a series that I chose to ignore.) I wrestled with the decision but in the end decided that my affection for my pets was immature. I dismissed my feelings and pursued the grown up course of action to become the wife of a gentile southern gentleman.

I drove to the shelter and offered my two precious pets up for adoption. After stoically surrendering them I sat in my car and cried harder and longer than any time before in my life, mostly because I knew I had just sent my aging, ugly and grouchy Princess to her death. The playful kitten had a chance of being adopted, but giving up this precious gift from my children was just as heart wrenching.

I gave up my pets for a man who never knew the pain I suffered over losing them. I can't blame him. It was I that should have stepped back and considered the options more carefully. If he truly had loved me then my two harmless felines would have been welcomed without consideration. After all, I hadn't disputed accepting his thirteen-year-old mostly-blind and incontinent Springer Spaniel as a piece of the baggage he came with. Taking in two cats who would always play second fiddle to this decrepit dog shouldn't have even been a consideration in our marital agreement.

Surrendering my pets was the first in a series of deep wounds that defined this season of my life. It took attorneys, psychologists, a strong church family, devoted friends and most of a year to pull the pieces of my life back together after I left the con man.

When I finally established a new normal I adopted a new cat, Cat. Unlike the last two, this cat's future with me was secure. Just like miners rely on canaries, I relied on Cat to detect toxic environments. I knew to step cautiously into any situation that might call for her surrender, and to run if there was anything in the air that might snuff out her life or mine.

The first challenge came from my mother. Thirteen years into her battle with cancer her health had deteriorated so much that she needed help. She and I had agreed in advance that I would relocate to her home in Michigan when that time came. We worked through the plans of my relocation, how we would merge our households, one delicate detail at a time. One day as she and I talked on the phone Cat's upcoming airline accommodations came up in the conversation. She blurted in disbelief, "You're not bringing the cat are you?"

"What?" I responded, stunned, "Of course I am." A moment of silence followed, and then I proclaimed, "If the cat can't come, then I can't come."

Bam. We had hit a wall. How could we have made it this far in our home merging process without addressing this critical assumption -- an assumption with a tripping wire that was nearly detonated by a canary-cat. She knew I was grieved by the fate of my previous cats. I assumed she knew how I felt about this one.

I wonder what I would have done if she would have called my bluff. Instead it turned out to be the first in a succession of compromises in our life and death experience together. It also turned out to be the best thing that ever happened to Cat. Within weeks of our arrival Genevieve was doting on her like she was a long-lost companion.

Cat quickly adjusted to the new routines: a teaspoon of cream in "Cat's" saucer each morning, afternoon naps on the sun-warmed Oriental rug beneath Genevieve's feet, and chin scratching on-demand anytime Cat hopped up in Genevieve's lap.

Cat responded to Genevieve's reprimands like a well-trained dog. And when I treated Cat with anything but tender touches and kind words, I was reprimanded by Genevieve as well.

After Genevieve's death and our return to Phoenix, Cat made it perfectly clear that she preferred her life in Michigan over the one in Phoenix. When I introduced her to the RV she inspected every nook and cranny as if looking for reasons to display her disapproval again. But she didn't. She took to her new home as if Genevieve herself had designed it just for her.

We had both found our new safe haven.

# { 7 }

# Drop Off

It's a beautiful summer day in Arizona. The temperature is expected to reach 114 degrees and the RV is scheduled for service and a pre-trip safety check at a local RV Repair Shop.

As soon as I finish my breakfast I load my bike into the trunk of my car, drive to the Big Toy Storage Lot, park, transfer the bike into the RV, and hitch the bare tow dolly on to the RV.

I pop into the driver's seat of the RV and maneuver it out of the narrow parking space, through the storage lot gates, and out onto the road. I'm feeling like a real motor home mama. And without the car loaded on the tow dolly, it feels as easy as driving a full size SUV.

But within minutes driving the RV on the narrow and congested city streets is unnerving, especially when road construction pylons narrow the lanes even further. In addition to workmen everywhere, I see a cop directing traffic up ahead. I obey his hand signals to continue through the intersection, but not without hearing a snap! – snap! coming from somewhere behind me. Immediately I check my mirrors for casualties and see only a pylon wobbling wildly in my wake. While thanking God that I haven't nailed a police officer I simultaneously wonder what damage I've done to the RV.

I make it to the shop, register with the desk attendant, turn over my keys, unload the bike and pedal away. It's not unusual for me to take seven mile hikes in the middle of the day during the summer. I like the sun on my skin and don't mind the heat. So I'm looking forward to my bike ride back to my car.

The first four miles go fairly smoothly, except for navigating through the road construction. The traffic is infinitely thicker than I've ever seen it on this stretch and heavy equipment workers are leveling what used to be road shoulders into road lanes. The heat from the cars and the dry dirt circulating in the air are fatiguing me more than I expected. I decide to turn off the main drag and ride the neighborhood streets the rest of the way. It's a longer but safer route.

I'm about five miles into the ride and for the first time in the twenty years I've lived in Arizona I feel the symptoms of heat exhaustion coming over me. My muscles are cramping. I'm chilled by the sweat on my body. Goosebumps cover my arms. I'm light headed, really light headed, and just conscious enough to recognize that this is not good.

I'm on a less traveled street than before but still in heavy and fast-moving traffic. I'm weak and nauseous.

Suddenly I spy a deep green lawn shaded by a massive green tree in front of a bank building on the other side of the street, across four lanes of traffic. The coolness of the deep green grass beckons me. With all the brain power I can muster I focus on it and pedal faster to get to it.

I twist my neck from side to side, scanning the lanes of traffic, searching for an opening. Quickly and cautiously I thread my way through cars and trucks to the median, then across the opposing lanes. If I can remain conscious for a few more feet, I'll make it to the green spot . . . where I can drop my bike . . . and drop into that cool deep green grass.

I'm close to fainting, but I've made it. I drop the bike and flop into the cool deep grass. Ahhhhh. I'll be okay if I can drop my body temperature a degree or two, grab my water bottle and take a drink. I'm still too lightheaded to reach it right now.

I feel a pinch on my ankle. Then another one on my calf. Then three more on that leg and now some more on the other leg too. Ants! Fire ants! The cool deep grass is home to a colony of fire ants. Their pinching bites feel like a mist of acid on my limbs. I jump up and start slapping my legs, dancing like a foot-stomping hillbilly trying to shake them from my skin. I'm quite a show for the bank employees watching from inside their windowed offices.

I wiggle and jiggle into the bank's paved driveway and grab my water bottle. The entire contents disappear down my throat in seconds flat and I'm back on my bike pedaling away. Not fully alert yet, but I've been snapped back into full consciousness by those darn ants.

A short while later I'm within a mile and a half of the Big Toys Storage Lot pedaling down a narrow dirt path between raging traffic and a heat-radiating cinder block wall. I'm safe. I slow my speed and am almost enjoying the ride when I notice that my back tire is just about flat. Thinking that it has just lost a bit of air, I continue on. I glance at my front tire and . . . oh no! It's just as flat! I've been sabotaged by thumb-tack-sharp, goat-head-shaped burrs from the pesky desert weed choking the path. Goat-head burrs are to my tires what the fire ants were to my skin.

Within another block I dismount, bow my head in surrender, and trudge on. I finally reach the storage lot gates and see my Saturn parked inside, like an oasis in the desert. I load my bike in the trunk, plop into the driver's seat and head home.

The RV will stay where it is until tomorrow. I need 24 hours to recuperate.

# { 8 }

# The Pickup

After yesterday's fiasco of dropping off the RV at the mechanic's, I wake up this morning to consider my options for picking it up. I go to my when-all-else-fails strategy — ask for help. I'm not very good at that, but my RV is already pushing me to use the when-all-else-fails strategy more than I am used to or comfortable with.

I ask my neighbor for a ride to the shop. Yes, of course she will help me. She grins at me with anticipation of the inevitable "I told you so" day. This is the same neighbor who told me I am crazy to want such a life. She and her husband had purchased a brand new completely decked out Mercedes travel van a few years prior and after one trip she demanded its return to the dealer.

The Mercedes was luxurious, but still cramped, and to take advantage of every inch of available space the unit's bed was stowed in the ceiling of the van and had to be lowered every evening before bed time. She absolutely couldn't deal with that (even though her husband managed the mechanics of it). The second thing that she had absolutely no tolerance for was having to empty black and gray water tanks, which, again, was her gentleman's responsibility. Living in an RV is not for everyone.

I have so much to learn about my new investment. I feel barely confident enough to drive the thing. I'm practically ignorant about towing the car, connecting to, and disconnecting from electrical power and plumbing systems. Running the generator, checking the oil, and maintaining the proper tire pressure in the dual tires are all activities far outside of my comfort zone. What regular maintenance checks can I do on my own? And how can I find competent mechanics to help me on the road? I'm paralyzed with fear when I think about all of this at the same time.

But the most important thing I have to learn is how to ask for help. Asking for a lift to the mechanic's shop is easy because at least I know the words. But black water, gray water, receiver hitch, suspension air bags - asking for help with these requires me to know what they are and how they operate. And then I have to communicate my need to someone who also understands their meanings and functions. I need to learn this new language.

My most basic struggle with my vehicle is the words that identify my vehicle. Is it an RV or a MH? Should I call it by its brand name or model name? By size, or by class? Instinctively I want to call it an RV but my brain rebuffs that word. I'm living in a recreational vehicle? A muddy old four-wheeler parked on a plywood floor and used as a bench to a red-neck-engineered plywood dining table come to mind. That's not how I live, and definitely not the image I want to convey to those asking about my comfortable abode.

Sitting in the mechanic's waiting area I ponder this. The room smells of man sweat and motor oil. Qualified mechanics ready my rig for the road. And listening to their chatter I learn the answer. All my anxieties are alleviated as the mechanics repeatedly refer to my vehicle with two simple words: "The Coach".

That's it! I live in a coach, a motor coach. Those words are so much more appealing than "RV". And when I ask someone for help with my motor coach they'll know that I don't live in a 5th wheel or a camper. And immediately they'll know that it's shaped like a bus rather than a van.

The desk man hands over my keys after I pay my bill. Today has been an easy day. Trained professionals have checked the engine and con-firmed that the coach is ready for the road. I've taken a small step forward by asking for help and I've expanded my vocabulary by two essential words. With each passing day I'm feeling more confident about taking on this coach life.

# { 9 }

# The Purple Park

Blogs written by home-on-wheels owners recommend that newbies like me make my virgin trip a short one:

> *"It gives you, the novice, a chance to adjust to the sounds of the coach on the road, become accustomed to the feel of the fully-loaded rig, and recognize the tug of the car dolly. Once settled, spend a night and day ensuring that the rig is loaded with essentials. Pick up gear, tools and supplies that were needed or forgotten, and dispose of any non-essential weight before moving on."*

Heeding their advice, I make a reservation at The Purple Park for the following night. It's 20 miles away and just off the interstate. The spotlights that shine on the entrance sign are as purple as the sign itself.

I pull into the park and I am enveloped in purple. Everywhere purple. Every building, every fence, every hook up post, even the walkways around the park are painted purple. Definitely won't forget this place.

I check-in at the park office and ease my coach into my assigned parking space. I'll be dry-docking (camping without utilities) tonight because I'm still too scared to try to hook up any of my systems. And I'm even more terrified to ask for help and expose myself as a completely uneducated novice. Fortunately I have battery power that allows me to turn on the lights and boil water in my electric kettle. I'll visit the purple bath house to brush my teeth tonight and shower in the morning.

I've let Cat out to explore and by the time my tea is steeped I hear her meow at the door. I let her in. She saunters past me and tracks red dust on the kitchen's vinyl floor. She nibbles down her evening meal and when she's done I notice more red dust around her nearly empty food bowl.

Next she plops herself down on the bed. The white coverlet is instantly tinged the same rusty red color. It's then I notice that the only thing that's not purple in this park is the dirt on the ground. It's rusty red. Rusty red sand that is easily embedded in the fur of a rolling-in-the-dirt feline.

Cat may not understand words but she responds to the tone of my voice the way a child does to a mother's. I point out the spots where she has deposited the rusty red grit and scold her. She acknowledges my pointed finger with a dismissive glance, assumes her napping posture, and shuts her eyes.

I ignore her blatant disregard and head outside to check out the park on my evening walk. My next door neighbor is tinkering outside of her camper. She and her husband have lived in the park since her husband's job relocation brought them here six months ago. She works out of her home office inside the 22' trailer. (And I think my home is small!) I pass by other transient inhabitants who smile and chat about their travels and adventures. I stroll back to the coach where I enjoy a comforting cup of instant chicken noodle soup.

Shortly after I finish eating I hear a knocking sound outside. I peek out my window and see the neighbor's husband gingerly tapping a bottle of wine on a tree's trunk behind their camper. He takes aim at the tree, powers the bottle toward the trunk, but stops just before the bottle makes contact. And then he disappears back into of the camper.

Thirty seconds later his wife is knocking on my door requesting a wine opener. She tells me that they had watched someone knock the bottle neck off a wine bottle using this tree-smacking technique. They agreed that he would attempt the stunt on his own but he chickened out at the last minute. It would be a shame to lose the fine nectar if he failed to execute the stunt successfully. She soon returns with my opener and a full glass of fine red wine for me.

The next morning I awake to discover that the pleasant night winds that lulled me into a deep and sound sleep were simultaneously depositing rusty red sand on every interior surface in the coach. Cat lounges outside under the front end of the coach while I clean what I can without running water. (Learning how to hook up the water just became a top priority.) As soon as I finish sweeping out the coach Cat takes one last roll in the rusty red dirt and hops back inside.

After showering, meeting a few more neighbors and completing a quick safety check, Cat and I pack up and head for higher elevation. Two hours away we pull into our next stop and rent a space in the shade of a grand old mesquite tree. Cat hops out, explores, and soon meows to come back in. Crispy dry leaves replace the rusty red dirt embedded in Cat's fur at the last stop. Obviously a rolling-in-the-dirt feline will bring the outside inside everywhere we go.

Cool crisp night air seeps through the window. I crawl into my cozy bed, pull the coverlet over my shoulder and thank God for the day. It's eerily quiet here and the familiar sounds of city traffic are non-existent.

Instead, the call of a hoot owl in the grand old mesquite tree lulls me to sleep.

# { 10 }

# Curves

With two trial nights under my belt I'm finally ready to spend a full day on the road. Today I will travel 250 miles from Phoenix, half way to Bayfield, Colorado where my sons and their families live. Bayfield will be my last familiar stop before moving on to parts unknown.

The Phoenix metropolitan area lies in the flat and wide Salt River Valley. Interstate 17, which heads north from the city, climbs out of the valley through a series of rolling hills. The elevation rises from barely above sea level to over 6,000 feet within 140 miles.

The highway is dotted with caution signs: "Sharp Curves", "Steep Grades", "Trucks Use Low Gear" and even "Runaway Truck Ramp Ahead". My favorite, particularly on a hot summer day, is: "Turn Air Conditioning Off To Avoid Overheating". I've traveled this road so many times over the past twenty years that I know these warnings like the back of my hand. The signs blur as I zip past them at 80mph.

But today everything feels different. I am a novice behind the wheel of a rig weighing slightly over 15 tons and five times as long as a mid-sized car. Without exercising extreme caution, I will be a hazard to myself and those around me. As I climb those hills the engine revs to a maximum speed of 45 mph; as I glide down them I am challenged to maintain that same comfortable speed. Cars line up behind me on the way up, and whiz by me on the way down. I'm an inconvenience, and I know it. But better safe than speedy.

About three quarters of the way up that 6,000 foot elevation climb I reach the section of highway that makes my toes curl. The two narrow lanes of northbound traffic make an eight-mile snaking descent into Verde Valley. Even in a car it's intimidating. In my super-sized rig it's downright terrifying. I pull into the area marked "Check Brakes Here" at the top of the hill. There I inspect my vehicle, climb back into my coach and pull out my copy of Beth Moore's Praying God's Word. It's a great collection of promises from the Bible packed neatly into one small paperback.

Promises of protection. Promises of safety. Promises of love, and a fulfilled future. I begin reading one promise after another, aloud, starting with the ones referring to the fulfilled future. (I have to be alive to have a fulfilled future, right?) But my pulse is still racing. I burst into tears. Preparing to cruise down this eight-mile hill feels like I'm jumping off a cliff.

Cat is poised attentively in front of me, inquisitively studying my face, confused by my show of hysterics. Her curious expression tells me that this breakdown is not normal, or appreciated. I must snap out of it and pull myself together. I've just read the promises, now I must believe them. I stand up, wipe the tears away from my face and begin pacing the length of the coach. With a steady voice I speak the promises out loud. I continue repeating each one of them until I can speak them as confidently as a politician delivering a campaign speech. And then I settle myself back into the driver's seat of my dream vehicle.

I fasten my seat belt, check my gauges, then my mirrors, and then cautiously pull out into the highway. The driver of a cherry red sports car traveling 80mph lays on his horn. He rattles the self-confidence I have just barely mustered. After a quick pick up in speed I shift the transmission into low gear and perch my foot on the brake pedal. The weight of the coach relentlessly pushes it down the hill. As the engine revs up the transmission holds the coach's speed in check. I press firmly on the brake to knock the speed back down to the lower end of the gear. I know from years of driving pickup trucks while towing trailers full of horses over mountain passes that this transmission-brake dance is what it takes to reach the bottom of a long steep decline . . . in one piece.

Again the coach surges in an effort to exceed the speed allowed by its own low gear. Again I apply firm pressure on the brake to bring it back into check. One curve down. Then the next. Another curve. Cars whiz by. I try to relax my fingers — they are clamped tightly on the steering wheel. I comfort the cat, "It's okay baby girl, it's okay." I know she doesn't have a clue about what's happening but by calming her I calm myself. Three more curves and I see the warning sign, "Steep Grade Next 2.1 Miles". A brief spurt of euphoria, I've already come six miles! But I'm not out of the curves yet. I take a deep breath. I silently repeat another promise to myself. And then I see the straight away nearing the bottom of the hill. I feel like a timid child who, after much coaxing from a loving parent, just skied down her first bunny hill.

I've made it! I exit the highway, pull into a truck parking area and pop outside to get some fresh air and let the adrenaline drain from my veins. My muscles feel like jello. I stumble around, taking in the vast high desert landscape surrounding me. Multi-mauve-colored sandstone buttes border it in every direction. The Verde River that meanders through this area is hidden deep in the canyon just north of where I stand. Its waters are critical to the survival of life in this arid zone. I think those promises are the same to my survival. I raise my arms in grateful appreciation of my safe delivery into this stunning valley.

Cat observes me from her dashboard perch complaining about her captivity with resentful meows. Once my pulse and breathing rate are back to normal I return to the coach, give her some reassuring rubs and resume driving the highway to the next valley.

I've just spent five hours driving what typically takes me about three. Not bad considering my novice status. My goal for today has been accomplished.

The day ends with a quiet campsite on a high desert mesa 6,000 feet above sea level. The sunset throws brilliant rays of orange, pink and purple across the horizon. The first evening star twinkles against the magnificent backdrop. I will rest well. I know tomorrow's roads are paved with promises.

# { 11 }

# Ax Murderers

A well-meaning relative expressed her concerns when I announced that I was taking on this unconventional lifestyle, "Aren't you scared to stay in those trailer parks? How do you know the people next to you aren't ax murderers?" She wouldn't have understood if I told her that I was much more concerned about concealing my identity as a naive rookie than my safety in the parks.

I think about this during my second day on the road while driving to Colorado. I suppose she has a point. Safety is important but with a bit of research and cautious consideration I know I can minimize the chances of foul play coming my way. I am excited to get to the Bayfield Riverside RV Park where I have reserved a space next to the creek.

The park owner greets me as I pull into the park's driveway. He directs me to follow him to my rented space. He is friendly and I feel comfortable enough to reveal my rookie status to him.

"Okay, I just want you to know that this is the first time I'll be hooking up to anything. I'm brand new to this." I confess.

"No problem. I'll help you hook up after we get you parked in your space. I'll guide you in," he offers.

He leads me to the spot where we unload my car and unhitch my car dolly. Then he maps out how I will turn the coach and back it into the space. Once it is turned and in position he places himself in line with my rear view mirrors and professionally directs me back into the proposed position. I follow his signals with pinpoint accuracy and am perfectly situated on our target spot with the first try. Then he helps me pull out cords and hoses all the while giving me tips for parking, traveling and what to do as the temperatures continued to drop.

"Now just a word to the wise," he cautions, "Take a feminine approach when touching anything inside or outside the coach. Use a gentle touch every time. There will always be plenty of opportunities to break things."

Within minutes I am connected to water, sewer and power and am informed that the propane truck will be here in the morning. All I need to do to get my tank filled is to wait outside and flag down the driver.

I reflect on his suggestion to use a gentle feminine touch. Obviously he is of a different mindset than my mechanic friend back in Arizona. When he saw me wrestling with my car dolly hitch he had advised, "Don't be afraid to bang on it! Whenever something is stuck, just bang on it with a mallet or hammer!" Looks like I'll have to learn when to handle things with a feminine touch and when to pound on it like a man.

The next morning I meet my nearest neighbor as we wait outside of our respective vehicles for the propane truck. He and his wife are Texans, long time motor home owners who regularly make a stop at this park en route to visit family in Wyoming and Montana every summer. I admit that I am on my maiden voyage and he assures me that I will love every bit of this lifestyle. The propane truck arrive, fills our tanks

# COACH LIFE

and continues on to the other campers. My neighbor and I bid each other good day.

The next morning this same neighbor knocks on my door and practically orders me to come over and "talk RV" with him and his wife. As I am putting on my shoes he doesn't head back to his motor home as I expect, but rather is striding purposefully to the opposite side of my coach. Once there he pops open all of my utility compartments. His wife hops out of their rig and falls into step right behind him. She introduces herself as she surveys the open compartments over his shoulder.

They silently critique my set-up with hmms and humphs and "oh my" looks between each other. Without waiting for permission they begin undoing hoses and cords and pipes, reconnecting them in a more streamlined fashioned. When they get to the waste pipes she takes the lead in adjusting the fittings. He turns to me and proudly announces, "She's the "Potty Expert."

"Yes, I'm the Potty Expert," she self-assuredly confirms.

When the necessary adjustments are completed they continue my lesson with instructions about carrying water when I'm traveling. They teach me how to fill and empty the tank, and how to use my water pump. They teach me how to optimize my gas mileage and still have all the comforts of modern plumbing available at all times.

Next they move on to the other side of my coach to show me how to operate my awning, and even more importantly, how to stow it properly. They share the story of how a rogue wind once tore their entire awning, frame and all, right off the side of their rig while they were traveling down the highway. (Apparently it's a fairly common occurrence since the guy who sold me the coach told me an almost identical story.) They suggest that I add some Velcro straps to hold the frame close to the vehicle during those windy travel days.

Finally, after assuring them three times that I don't need help with anything else, they invite me to their rig for a tour and a visit. I can tell it's going to be nice inside because it's shiny new outside. And of course it is. When I step inside I hardly feel like I'm in a vehicle at all. The four pop-outs make it as wide as an apartment and with the cherry cabinets, a 42" flat screen tv, porcelain potty and king sized bed, it's as luxurious as a four-star hotel room.

We chat about our families and interests. I'm surprised that they are as addicted to thrift store shopping and garage-sale-ing as I am. They tell me stories about the fun places they've visited and the beautiful sites they've seen. We laugh about the rookie mistakes they made in the early years and they offer resources that will prevent me from making the same mistakes. Finally, they encourage me to join an RV club, specifically one that cater to singles. We exchange calling cards and promise to keep in touch. They invite me to visit their home in Denton, Texas anytime I am "in the neighborhood". This lovely couple, my new friends (not ax murderers), will leave early tomorrow morning to return there for the winter. We say our farewells. I leave the comfort of their abode and return to my own.

The crisp autumn night air has chilled my coach to a perfect sleeping temperature. I reach over to close and lock my kitchen window and SNAP! I look down and chuckle. A portion of the broken plastic latch rests in my palm. My first lesson on "using a feminine touch" is now complete.

# { 12 }

# The Bath House

I'm staying in this gorgeous park along the banks of the Pine River just outside of Bayfield, in the southwestern corner of Colorado, for the next two weeks.

Over 30 years ago I settled not far from where the coach is parked now. I attended college here, Fort Lewis College, also known as the "Campus in the Sky". I met and married a cowboy husband here, and birthed two sons. We raised horses, goats, chickens, ducks and a few other animals from time to time.

We lived in a community of ranchers who welcomed our help during their spring cattle drive. We'd saddle up our horses and help them drive their herd to high mountain meadows. There the cattle would fatten up over the summer and in late fall we'd help round up the herd and drive it back down to its valley home. When we weren't riding to check cattle we sometimes rode for days at a time through the Weminuche Wilderness on trails that crisscrossed the Continental Divide. It was a wonderful life in the magical land of quaky aspens, evergreen pines, crystal clear streams and azure blue skies.

It was also a difficult time. The challenges of living a life steeped in century-old traditions took its toll on the young marriage and we divorced. What's left of that life is planted on either side of this Bayfield Riverside RV Park. Our two sons live a few miles to the west. My ex-husband and his wife of ten years live a few miles to the east. The ex-in-laws have extended an open invitation to me to stay at their home any time and for as long as I would like. But I'm enjoying my cozy coach home too much to take them up on their offer on this visit.

The park is peaceful. The first of Colorado's majestic autumn colors dot the grounds like gourds hidden on a golf course. Spots of saffron yellow, scarlet red and chartreuse appear on tree branches and bushes, and on the creek in the thin early morning ice as if they are pressed in a floating mosaic. Deer are plentiful and peacefully graze on the last green grasses of the year. The air is perfumed with the sweet fragrance of cottonwood trees. Sleeping to the sound of the river is better than all the other things I love about this park . . . until I visit the Bath House.

My coach has a full size shower stall. I can take a shower any time I want. The day I picked up the coach from the tattooed Harley-riding Christian he instructed me to take "Navy" showers in it. "To make sure that you don't run out of hot water," he said, "you should rinse, turn off the water, lather up, and turn the water back on to rinse again."

Brrrrr. I'm definitely not cut out for the Navy. I've tried it several times already and although it's not exactly my idea of a pleasant shower it serves its purpose. After all I did expect to go without some of the luxuries of a permanent home in this thing.

I'm still trying to figure out how long my eight gallons of water will last – also wondering how much propane it takes to heat it. Running out of hot water mid-shower when I'm all suds up is scarier than coming face to face with an ax murderer. I'm extremely frugal with my hot water. I light the water heater just ten minutes before I'm ready to take a shower and turn it off as soon as I get out. To date I have not yet run out of hot water. . . and, I still haven't seen an ax murderer either.

This morning I look out the window and observe the first hard frost of the season. My propane heater is running and it's toasty warm in here, but a continual chill seeps through the floor. I'm not sure I'm up for the Navy shower this morning so I grab soap, towel and a washcloth and head to the Bath House. It's a quick cold sprint across the creek bridge but once inside the Bath House I'm so glad to be there. The room is warm, and well-lit, spacious, and squeaky clean. The shower stalls are large, furnished with benches and strong shower heads. I turn the shower valve to the highest setting. Steam envelopes me as I step into the full-flowing stream of piping hot water and luxuriate in one of the longest, dreamiest, best showers ever!

No more navy showers for me. This girl's going full on civilian in the Bath House from now on.

# { 13 }

# Notes on an Evening Walk

Bayfield, Colorado
Incorporated in 1906
Population:  2,087
Land Area:  1.08 square miles

Tonight I walk from one end of Bayfield to the other. It's barely a mile.

I see a couple cruising Main Street . . . on their horses.

I see a winter's worth of firewood stacked on the front porch of a tiny house. It has the unwelcome appearance of a primitive stockade fence rather than the heart-warming hospitality of the hearth fire it will fuel through the winter.

Further down the street I see a black and white goat grazing in the front yard of a turn of the century home, mowing the lawn no doubt.

I see two young boys in a front yard, trying their best to load a bike on an old rusty red wagon. They see me walking by and one declares to the other, "We sure could use some help, couldn't we?" And while both glance my way the other replies back to his friend, "Yep, sure could!"

Responding just as if that was my cue in a movie scene I help them load the bike. As soon as it's loaded their little cherub faces turn up towards me and clearly pronounce, "Thank you," in unison.

Boys at that kindergarten age are so precious. How quickly they will turn into young men.

I know. I've seen it happen to my own.

# { 14 }

# Stubborn

Today Cat and I are practicing stubborn-ness. Being stubborn.

Every day she refuses to eat the last little bit of dry food in the bottom of her bowl. So, I have to choose between throwing it away, and scolding her to clean her plate before I fill the bowl again. Although she's not quite finished, she wants me to top it off. I stubbornly ignore her begging meows for more. There are starving stray kitties right outside our door, and I have to throw food away? Nonsense! She refuses to eat, and I refuse to give in.

I am resolute.

Cat's meows are persistent.

Stubborn.

Both of us.

# { 15 }

# I'm An Elf

Adios Bayfield Riverside RV Park! I'm unhooked, packed up and on the road again.

Across the snow-covered southwestern Colorado mountains and valleys, through the undulating canyon and butte landscapes of New Mexico, across the Llano Estacado of Texas, through the cattle and oil fields of Oklahoma, and into the southeastern corner of the Sunflower State, Cat and I arrive at our new destination: Coffeyville, Kansas.

What? You've never heard of it? Well then I guess I'm not the only one who'll learn a thing or two from my traveling adventures.

So, yes, Coffeyville. It's not exactly one of those places that RVers consider a coveted destination. But BuyItOnline.com has a million-square-foot warehouse here and employs over 800 of what they call "Seasonal Campers" to help their permanent employees process orders during the busy Christmas season. An hourly wage, rig parking, utilities, BuyItOnline.com discounts, employee giveaways and an end-of-the-season bonus are included in their deal. Living among so many like-minded people is just the real-world educational experience I am look-ing for. So I applied and they called.

I start my new job as a BuyItOnline.com Seasonal Camper on Thurs-day. I and all the others are the updated versions of Santa's elves. We sort, count, stow, pick, and send all those items that you so conveniently pop in your shopping cart with a couple of keystrokes and a few clicks of a mouse during the Christmas season.

Not so effortless for us however. During my interview the BuyItOnline.com representative informed me that I could expect to work ten hour shifts, regularly lift up to fifty pounds, and walk 5-15 miles a day. "The work is physically challenging," he stated.

Okay, yep, I agreed that I was capable of fulfilling those require-ments. In fact it sounded like I might even shed one or two of the extra pounds on my hips in the process. All that fun will begin on Thursday. First I have a chance to meet a few of my neighbors who are also work-ing for BuyItOnline.com.

I met my next door neighbor, Joe, the minute I arrived. He greeted me with an enthusiastic, "Hello Neighbor!" and just like any good neighbor would, he jumped right out of his rig to help me unload my car, hook up my utilities and level the coach. As we worked he told me what it's been like since he arrived here ten days ago.

He's been on the job at BuyItOnline.com for a week and tells me how rigorously they control break times, how serious they are about clocking in and out of your shift at the scheduled times and how gruel-ing the work really is.

"The hiring manager wasn't kidding when he explained how long and hard the days would be," Joe declares, "I've got stiff and swollen knees. My hips ache. My muscles are sore and I'm dog tired from work-ing graveyard hours."

Joe is a disabled Navy vet who has lived out of his half-million-dollar rig for the past 13 years. He tows his jeep, his Harley and his golf clubs in an enclosed trailer wherever he goes. He's had a plethora of Work-Camping positions that all have two things in common: a comfortable climate and plenty of golf courses nearby. He's worked as a campground host in the Pacific Northwest, a mechanic on Padre Island, and a golf course groundskeeper in multiple golf destinations through the southwestern states.

He has perfected the art of living the gypsy life. The accouterments of his fully outfitted rig include a well-worn guitar, a prodigious repertoire of camp songs, and a story-telling singing style that keeps fellow campers entertained for hours around his propane-powered campfire.

His wife, Josephine, just arrived today in her own modest camper with the couple's miniature Yorkie, Bayley. The tiny dog stakes a claim to her newest territory in and around Josephine's Class C camper and Joe's Class A motor home and then prances right into my coach to have a look around. Cat is bewildered. Then perturbed. Cat liked our new location until the dog arrived. She glares at me like a belligerent teenager.

Josephine, also a retired Navy vet, has joined Joe here to earn a bit of Christmas cash and spend some time together. They've been married for over 20 years and have refined their caravan lifestyle to strike a balance between their separate interests and their highly valued time together. She has plans to replace the toys in his enclosed trailer with a hot tub. We laugh together at her longing for a whirlpool bath on wheels.

For right now they are parked hood-to-hood in the same pull-through space next to me and go back and forth between both rigs. That means I can't see anything past their 60 foot wall of tindominium from my south-facing windows. Not exactly ideal, but probably the best neighbors in the place.

Two couples in two brand new state-of-the-art motor homes (the million-dollar versions) are parked behind me. The two meticulously maintained wives, Beverly and Patricia, sit in upgraded patio chairs among the potted plant gardens bordering the front of their homes. They sip wine from Riedel crystal glasses.

"How lovely it is to see you sipping from real wine glasses," I tell them as I stroll by on my evening walk. They giggle and reply, "We may have gypsy kitchens but that doesn't mean we have to live without china and crystal."

I agree with them. When my sister passed up taking my mother's good china and I unexpectedly ended up with it, I decided I would actually use it rather than keep it safely packed away for most of my life as Genevieve had done. So I replaced my everyday kitchen dishes with it. I was stunned at how the change exalted even the simplest food choices. Slurping cereal from a bone china bowl with a sterling silver spoon made me feel like I was eating from room service in an upscale Bed and Breakfast Inn.

I tell the two meticulously maintained wives in their potted plant garden that bringing my mother's china on the road with me was just too impractical, that I instead decided to purchase some designer melamine dish-ware for the coach before I left.

"Nonsense!" the brunette, Patricia, scolds, "Get a few pieces out of storage and use them in the coach. If you happen to break one, you can always replace it with another. What good is it to anyone in storage?" I saw her point. Packing them away again was denying myself the simple pleasure I had discovered by using them. What on earth was I thinking when I boxed up the china and made a special trip to the big box store to purchase cheap replacements?

We chat on and they recite their personal profiles to me. The brunette's husband is a retired CIA agent, the blonde's, owner of a small airline company. The husbands plan to work at BuyItOnline.com until a few days before Christmas. The wives will relax and explore the local area, which more than likely is code for "shop" from the looks of things. Then they will travel to their children's homes where they will spend the holidays before heading south for the remainder of the winter. The men are avid golfers and have already lined up their next workcamper gigs as pseudo groundskeepers for an exclusive course in southern Arizona. We bid each other a good evening and I continue my walk.

Cat tentatively follows along behind me, slinking safely from one camper's underbelly to the next as we make our way down the park drive. I meet a single woman next, living in a camper not much bigger than a tin can. She tells me she is running away from a crazy husband, barely surviving, and not sure how she will manage living in her inadequate vehicle in the frigid winter weather. As we speak she cuts strips of foil insulation to stick into her windows. Not only will it be cold in her tiny home, it will be dark too.

I walk a bit further and run into a couple living in a 22' camper with three greyhounds. Who came up with that plan? At times Cat feels like too much of a commitment in my small space! Then I meet a family of five living in a camper about the same size as the greyhounds' home. The disheveled collection of housewares, tools and toys outside of their door appear to be remnants of a recent eviction.

Back at my coach a man looking like a red-haired Paul Bunyan is walking his prissy French Bulldog. I comment on the dog's leather spike-studded collar and immediately the lumberjack-size man proudly introduces his stud, Dually, (you know, like the slang word for dual rear wheel pickup trucks).

"Ma waf's got a matchin' one. Dif'rent litter, same fine pedigree," he declares in a thick southern drawl, "Her dog's name is Daisy Duke." He continues on about the dogs, "They's bloodlines goes all the way back to France."

Turns out this proud Texan is here with his wife on their maiden voyage as well. They live in a fifth wheel toy-hauler that they got for next to nothing. (Toy-haulers are campers with built-in garages for hauling toys, like four wheelers and motorcycles. Fifth wheels are campers that are towed by a pickup truck equipped with a special hitch mounted in the truck's bed.) He continues on and on and on about what a nice unit it is.

What a variety of people and tales contained in this park. Already I have met an entire storybook of colorful characters and I haven't even starting working yet.

# { 16 }

# Simple Pleasures

I've discovered a few things I cannot live without in my simple tiny life in the coach. One is a great haircut and color. Another, restaurants that operate 7 days a week.

Coffeyville is located in a "dry county", which means that you can't buy alcohol on Sundays — not in stores and not in restaurants. And therefore restaurants that sell alcohol are closed on Sundays.

Sundays are my day off. On my day off I look forward to a great dinner at a fine local diner. I also look forward to indulging myself by purchasing a glass of fine wine to drink with it. But here in Coffeyville on my day off I get neither. I'm fully capable of preparing a five-star meal for myself at home, but rarely keep a bottle of wine in the pantry. Preparedness is critical and not entirely a strength of mine.

I guess it was a mistake to venture this far from home with gray roots because when I ask the camp host for a salon recommendation she directs me to the Walmart salon without hesitation. She could have recommended one in town, "But you need an appointment there," she laments, "The gal at Walmart cuts my hair just fine."

I'm glad to hear that she is satisfied with her cut. She has that wavy kind of hair that easily hides imprecise scissor cuts made by the untrained hands of an amateur. Mine, on the other hand, is mousy fine, straight as a ruler's edge and shames any hair designer who's cut is not strategically executed. But, with a sales pitch like hers I am forced to remember where I am. I realize that asking for a better option would be insulting.

So I make my way down to the Walmart salon, settle into a seat and rattle off a few basic suggestions and requests. The stylist responds with befuddlement. I do not mention my graying roots. She doesn't either. Twenty minutes later I walk out of the salon with my freshly-cut-dripping-wet hair and a plan to dye my own roots in the privacy of my own coach. The next day I apply a box of do-it-yourself hair color to my roots . . . without dripping a drop of the staining liquid on any surface in the coach. Another coach life success story!

I'm two weeks into the job and feeling terribly out of shape. My knees hurt, my hips hurt, my leg muscles burn continually. I am sleep deprived. I have never worked graveyard shifts and adjusting to this vampire schedule is proving more difficult than I expected. I have no idea how BuyItOnline.com's Seasonal Campers that are ten or twenty years older than I am do it, particularly those who are returning for their second, third, and even sixth year at this very location. I see one couple regularly on my shifts. They are both pushing 80. This is their sixth year here and they stride these warehouse walkways grinning from ear to ear. He's a retired pastor and she is a retired nurse. In between travels to their children's homes throughout the country and their winter home in Florida they stop here for six weeks each year for endurance training.

They tell me it's their way to give an extra boost to their regular physical fitness regimen. If my body is in that kind of shape at that age, I suppose I'll be grinning too. Right now the only thing that feels youthful about me is my fake brunette hair.

I speed walk the promised five to fifteen miles a day. I'm also lifting, squatting and climbing stairs for ten hours a day, five days a week. The Paul Bunyan Texan with the prissy French Bull Dog is on the same team as I and we beat the monotony of our work tasks by competing with each other for recognition as the fastest worker in our department.

Each of us is assigned a hand-held computer unit that tells us which products to pull, stock or count in the warehouse's inventory. It also records where we are, what we're doing, how long it takes to do it, and how quickly we move to the next place in the warehouse to do the next task on its list. Our handy-dandy hand-held computers then condense and compile all that information into neatly arranged reports that are printed and posted in our departments throughout our shifts. The Paul Bunyan Texan and I are always at the top of the list. I suppose I wouldn't hurt so badly if I wasn't so competitive, but the most difficult part of the job by far is the boredom associated with the monotony. And the competition is the best antidote.

I've considered the sad state of my aching knees and continuous fatigue and more than once thought about leaving this place and getting a job elsewhere. However, today I am wearing pants that are a size smaller than those I arrived in. And my colored hair makes me look as young as I want to feel.

I will stay to the end.

# { 17 }

# Jeremiah 29:11

It's been a month since I became a BuyItOnline.com Seasonal Camper and the first weekend off that I've actually felt "normal". My body has turned aches, pains and constant fatigue into strength and vigor. I'm able to spend my free time relaxing instead of rehabilitating. I'm able to focus some of my attention on renewing my mind and my spirit.

I lounge on my sofa, sipping Earl Grey tea from my favorite mug. My legs are tucked under a soft lavender blanket, my Bible open and resting on my lap. Cat is curled deep into her own plush pillow next to me. The electric heater hums harmoniously with the gentle rain tapping on the roof. We're nestled in a cocoon of comfort.

My coach is parked with 75 other coaches of BuyItOnline.com Seasonal Campers in a field that borders the main drag of an industrial park in which the BuyItOnline.com warehouse is located. Semi-trucks pass by constantly. It's anything but a haven of peace and tranquility.

I look down at the open page.

*"For I know the plans I have for you," declares the Lord, "plans to prosper you and not to harm you, plans to give you hope and a future. . ."*

I've believed in God for a long time, and Jesus has been a friend of mine since childhood. But not in a "what a friend we have in Jesus" churchy way - more like a knowing-in-my-soul way. We moved around a lot when I was growing up. By the time I graduated from high school I had attended eight schools. That's more than 1.5 schools every two years. It's hard to make friends when your papa's a rolling stone and your mama's rolling along with him. I was a child in need of a dependable, consistent relationship. Often friendless, I thought of Jesus like an invisible friend, a sort of protective older brother.

I knew stories in the Bible. But it took decades of re-reading and applying them to my life before I truly learned the value of the promises written within it. Jeremiah 29:11 happens to be one of my favorites. Prosper me? Give me a future? On dark nights, in an anxious state I've cried out, "Show me this promise now!" At times it's been hard to believe, but hindsight has verified the truth of these words time and time again.

And today, again, I see it clearly.

This morning as the sun broke over the horizon I rode my bike along a quiet prairie road where crickets sang and earthy farmland scents nourished my soul the way food from the farm feeds my hunger.

The seedy bare-bones industrial warehouse that I quick-pace through has been transformed into a community village. Up each staircase and around each corner I see faces of the workcampers and permanent employees that are now friends, part of a community that reaches across all parts of the country.

Last night, here in Coffeyville amazingly enough, I saw my first mountain lion ever. After living most of my life in the west, in the lion's natural habitat, I recognized the shape immediately as the cat streaked across the road just inches ahead of my car's front bumper.

The hoots of a night owl are my lullaby every night as I cuddle into my warm, soft bed. And my cat is a continual source of companionship and comedy as she learns this new way of life with me.

I'm safe, and secure. My needs are met and I want for nothing.

I'm living my dream.

That's the thing about God's promise. It doesn't always look like we think it should. From the outside looking in it may seem as if God hasn't even noticed me, let alone prepared prosperity and a future for me. But to me it couldn't be clearer.

# { 18 }

# A Preacher's Son

There's no end to the characters that I've met in this community of BuyItOnline.com's Seasonal Campers. Take the Paul Bunyan Texan for example. He's known as "Red" in our community. He spend afternoons under the awning of his camper, sitting in his chaise lounge reading his Bible and sipping on a Texan-sized rum and coke. His daddy, a Baptist preacher, always told him, "Son, don't matter which way a person studies the Book so long as they's a-studying it!" Red follows his daddy's advice "religiously".

His wife is not nearly as impressed with the Good Book. She's equally interested in the riches of this world and when they are going to reappear in their life again. She waffles between fussing about enduring these unacceptable living conditions and bragging about how hard Red toiled to win her and eventually lead her to the altar.

She and he had both been married more than once before so there were plenty of prenuptial negotiations prior to their union, one being that he would build a house to her specifications and liking. Turns out the house was built on what the Good Book would call a "foundation of shifting sand". Within a few short years the couple lost the house and hocked the ring. They are practically penniless now except for their home-on-wheels which was secured for a fraction of its value. "I stole it!" Red boasts to offset her tales of defeat.

Despite their financial woes and hen-pecking banter, it's clear they have a Texan-sized love for each other. Pass by their awning and you'll likely see him crafting a piece of furniture for her, or her preparing a special meal for him -- or both of them empathetically sharing stories, laughs, and tears with workcampers that gather around them like bees to blue bells.

Their tales of Texan-sized struggles are wrapped with comedic twists and punctuated with Red's attempts to weave a Biblical promise into each and every one of them. Their lives are deeply rooted in home-grown Texan hospitality and fertilized with fun-loving goodness. What else would you expect from a Preacher's son and his wife?

# { 19 }

# Am I Capable?

A suitor of mine, who had never been married, labeled me an unacceptable marriage partner because I've been divorced three times. Divorced 3 times? I can see your mouths dropping as you read this. Yes, it's true. I'm not proud of it, but it's a part of who I am.

So, what's your first question? --Why?

Or "What's wrong with her?"

Do you still like me?

When it happens in Hollywood, its titillating news. We spend our money on magazines to read about it. We discuss it. We take sides. We defend our favorite. We decide who does and doesn't deserve whom. But when it happens in our own circle, it's different.

I was raised on the American girl fantasy, longing for that perfect man to marry me and carry me off into the sunset to live happily ever after. I had no idea what marriage was all about when I came of age to consider the option. In fact, once I was old enough to consider it an option I barely understood how to live as a responsible single adult. I never learned the relationship skills required to successfully navigate marital territory. I'm not sure how or why, but I remained clueless.

So, I had to experiment. Instead of long courtships I opted for eloping after a few dates. I chased after a dream instead of seeing the reality in front of me.

Each marriage had its own unique challenges. Each divorce was painful, and left deep scars on me, my children and my extended family. Each experience made me stronger, and wiser. I became less judgmental and more compassionate; less arrogant and more humble; less defensive and more accepting.

I began studying the tenets of marriage, what makes a solid foundation, how to choose a mate, what faith communities and family counselors and God have to say about the whole matter. I started observing married couples and identifying real-life behaviors that encourage and hinder marital bliss. Now I understand where I went wrong. Now I realize how much intention it requires and how little I was willing to do to make a marriage work.

I have the utmost reverence for those who have stuck with this weighty commitment to each other. I'm absolutely giddy when I have the opportunity to share company and conversation with couples who have worked at it for 30, 40, 50 years or more. I know it's not easy . . . we're all flawed. But I can't imagine anything better than sharing happily ever after together on this earth.

I've studied marriage. I've learned what it's all about. Now I know it means living day in and day out with the same imperfect human being and doing your best, as another imperfect human being, to love that being as unconditionally as you possible can.

I'm an imperfect human being with a questionable record and the training to improve my odds. Would you bet on me?

# { 20 }

# Diggin' Out

My stint at BuyItOnline.com is done. I collect my end-of-season bonus, pack up the coach, say goodbye to all my new friends and pull out of Coffeyville two days before Christmas. I head back to Bayfield, Colorado, one of my many homes away from home to visit family and friends for a few weeks. Another perk of coach life is full control of my own schedule, including holiday breaks like the ones I remember as a school girl.

I love Colorado winters, sunshiny days, mornings glistening with ice-glazed tree branches and evening skies lit up with warm hues of cheery pink and sherbet orange. But this Colorado winter is unseasonably cold. The crisp mountain air hurts when it slaps my unprotected skin. I and my coach despise the below normal frigid temperatures.

Instead of struggling with freezing water lines, outrageous heating costs and constant complaints from a chilled feline, I've abandoned the coach at one friend's ranch and am staying with another. I've enjoyed my sabbatical but now it's time to make my way to Diablo Stadium in Tempe, Arizona for Major League Baseball Spring Training Season.

Today is pre-departure day. I will conduct safety checks and prepare for the 500-mile drive.

The coach is parked at the end of a snow-packed homemade country driveway. I remove all the snow that has piled up around it, in front of it and on top of it, and then hop inside to turn over the engine and let it run while I finish the rest of my chores. I unpack my suitcase and return my toiletries to the bathroom cupboard. I fill the pantry and fridge with groceries that I picked up on the way here. Everything is stashed away neatly and completely. I'm ready to call it a day. I'll have an easy start for a full day of travel tomorrow.

I arrive back at the coach early the following morning. Cat eagerly jumps out of the car and into the coach. Quickly she assumes her departure position. She hunkers deep down in the feather pillows on my bed in the very back of the coach. This is her standard starting position for every trip now. But within an hour she'll make her way up front where she'll sprawl out in the middle of the dashboard, observing the road like a captain on the bridge of a ship.

I take my place in the driver's seat, turn the key, and . . .wah-la! Nothing happens. There is no sound. The engine is silent. Only a click of the ignition switch. The unseasonably cold night has zapped my minimally charged battery. The upside: I will finally be able to use the Roadside Service I've been faithfully paying for on my insurance policy.

I make the call and minutes later Wayne of Bo Dean's Repair Service is on his way out to help me. I sit down on my bed next to Cat and think for a minute. I'm actually due for a new battery. If I can make it in to town, pick up a battery, and make it back to the coach in the 20 minutes it takes for Wayne to get out here I can probably talk him into helping me install it free of charge. I pop into my car and zip into town to grab a new battery. I get back just as Wayne pulls in next to the coach in his sparkling clean auto-mechanic-shop-on-wheels.

Wayne is slim, tall and cowboy handsome, dressed in brand new black Carhartt coveralls. He speaks with a western drawl that could calm a mama grizzly bear defending her cubs. My delayed start frustrations melt away as he gently reassures me, "Aww, don't you worry 'bout nothin'. I'll get you going' right away ma'am."

I tell Wayne about the new battery. "Well, you know we're not supposed to do nothin' but a jump," he says, "But seein' as how you got it here I reckon I can get it in place for you."

He pulls the old battery out. And then I hear a noncommittal "Huh".

"Now darlin', sorry to tell you but you got yourself the wrong kinda battery. You got a new top mount battery and this here calls for a side mount deal."

Huh. Rushed into town for nothing. Worse than nothing since now I have to return this battery and buy another one. Wayne leaves and I surrender to the fact that I won't be leaving today.

The next morning, I install the new battery. I'm filled with confidence as I plop into the driver's seat and turn the key, but . . . again, the uncooperative engine is silent . . . I feel deflated. This cold weather has snapped something in the ignition system and I'm hoping it's something insignificant.

I leave Cat in the coach and drive my Saturn back into town, to Bo Dean's Repair Shop to see what Wayne might have to say about the silence. Wayne's out, but the guys in the shop start spitting out solutions like chewing tobacco. "Could be a starter," says one, "Did you bang on the starter with a hammer? Sometimes that solves the problem." (Now we're back to banging on things.)

"Can you start your generator?" queries another, "Sometimes if your house batteries are charged you can start your generator and then start the engine off of that."

And then the quiet guy sipping coffee, perusing the local newspaper and surveying the situation over the rims of his reading glasses from behind the cashier desk says, "You can get it towed here and we can help you with it." Yeah, I saw that coming.

But even if I wanted to, towing the coach is hardly an option. It is readily positioned for me to drive it straight out of its parking space, but it's not an easy exit. I still have to maneuver it down a half mile of slippery snow-packed winding old homemade country driveway. Bo Dean's fancy shop-on-wheels can do plenty of things but towing that coach down that driveway is not one of them.

I decide to call my Road Side Service again and request another battery jump. It can't hurt to try one more time. But when I make my request that's not the way they see it. "Oh so sorry, we only allow one jump. After that you must have it towed," the agent tells me naturally assuming that it's as easy as hitching a wagon to a mule.

Hmmm . . . okay. What now?

First I decide to find shelter from the cold. I drive to a friend's house nearby where she brews up a pot of tea while I review my options and check out local mobile repair services online. I dial each one's number praying that I will find one sweet or desperate mechanic who is willing to come out and fix my coach in the single-digit temperatures and snow. I sure don't want to do it myself in this cold weather. I don't even want to wait for the fix-it man while he fixes it either. After a dozen calls, I finally find a mechanic who is up to the challenge. He promises to come . . . in ten days!

Surrendering again to my stranded status I return to the coach to pick up Cat. Yes, she's still in traveling position, hunkered down in the pillows and chilled to the bone. I make one last attempt to turn the ignition key and . . . wah-la! It starts! The engine is running! (I guess it was the "feminine touch" that did it this time.)

I'm free to leave. With new found hope I ease out of my parking space and load my car on its tow dolly. The coach slips, slides and bounces down the caddy wompus drive, across the cattle guard and between the mirror ponds that border the last section of the slippery snow-packed homemade country driveway.

I make it out onto the dry and clear highway late in the afternoon. Wayne, Bo Dean, and erroneous battery purchases are all forgotten in the euphoria of this unexpected freedom. The coach warms and Cat lets out an approving "meow" from the dashboard.

Free at last, and on the road again.

# { 21 }

# Stop 1: Ringing in My Ear

I cross the Colorado/New Mexico state line just as the sun drops far enough in the sky to shine directly into the upper portion of my windshield. I know I won't make it to my intended stopping point for the day and instead consider "Plan B" options. I could push myself to drive well into the night and *maybe* find a suitable place to pull over once exhaustion sets in. Or, I could go with the flow of this slow and steady travel day and opt for a sightseeing stop instead. I fight my natural urge to press on and exit the highway toward Window Rock, Arizona. I am finally going to see the window that Mother Nature carved out of rock.

The town itself is tiny, located in a remote corner of Arizona, northwest of Gallup, New Mexico. It appears sleepy, primitive and poor. But it's not. What seems to be a sparsely populated ranching community that the 21st century left behind is actually the capital seat of the largest Reservation in the United States, that of the Navajo Nation of North America. Tribal government officials in tribal government offices managing tribal affairs cause the town's permanent population of 2,000 to swell to over 20,000 during business hours each week.

But on the weekends Window Rock returns to its peaceful state on the high desert, hemmed in by sandstone buttes and spires that glow with brilliant hues of gold, alabaster, and amethyst in the stark southwestern sun. Rugged canyons flank the roads in and out of town. The colors of an impending sunset ooze across the horizon as I cruise the slow and arduous route toward the Navajo Veteran's Memorial Park where the actual Window Rock is preserved and protected.

As I pull into the Park I hear the tinkling of small bells like delicate wind chimes welcoming me. I maneuver through the narrow park drive and catch my first glimpse of the Window Rock. It rest in the saddle of a sandstone wall that's been cracked, curved and creased by water and wind over millions of years. Even from this distance I can practically feel the crystal blue sky shimmering through the unobstructed red stone window. I direct my attention back to driving and pull the coach into a vacant tour bus parking space.

I hike the short distance required to stand next to the enormous window. The jingling bells are silent now. I hear only the dusty winds whistle as they swirl through this sacred space. I pause, take in the tranquility of the place and the sky, and peacefully stroll back to my vehicle.

Back at the coach Cat waits impatiently for me . . . as usual. I climb into the driver's seat and slowly ease the coach out of the parking space. As I coast down the drive I hear the tinkling bells again. I stop in front of the Park Office, get out and look around for wind chimes. I don't see any anywhere.

Huh. Coincidentally, now that the coach is stopped the sounds of jingling bells have stopped too. I walk around the coach to see if I can locate the source. I giggle when I discover that what sounded like a gentle wind chime is actually a loose chain on my car dolly. As I curl under the axle of the dolly on my hands and knees to reattach the safety chain I give thanks that this dream adventure summons my full attention to every moment and every detail of it.

# { 22 }

# Stop 2: Know Your Limits

After my sightseeing stop at Window Rock I head to a local diner for an authentic Navajo Taco. Homemade Indian Fry Bread piled high with beans, chili meat and cheese, garnished with lettuce, tomato and onion. Just what a body needs when it's chilly outside and nearly bedtime.

I could continue driving for another hour or two and sleep in the coach but temperatures will bottom out in the teens tonight and I'd rather not fight the cold. I'm looking forward to a warm bed and a good night's sleep so I exit the freeway on the east side of Gallup, pull off into a parking lot and check out motel options on the internet. I find a good rate at one on the west side of town so I pull out of the parking lot and continue toward my destination on the frontage road. I decide to take the slower narrower route there instead of getting back on the highway. I've had enough of interstate driving and just want to get my oversized vehicle to its resting spot without cautiously switching lanes in 70mph traffic to do it.

Nine pm and it's a frigid 16 degrees in Gallup. Three quarters of the way to the motel I approach an underpass, and slam on the brakes. The warning sign indicates a 13'2" clearance.

How tall is my rig? Can I make it? I check the vehicle stats on the wall sticker next to me. I frantically flip through the owner's manual looking for the number. I am in the middle of the road and have to know if I can make it through that concrete frame.

I decide not to chance getting stuck in the underpass. But turning around won't be easy. I'm on a shoulder-less and narrow two lane road. Reversing directions will require unloading the car and unhooking the tow dolly, then ratcheting the 32' coach into position with multiple full range steering wheel maneuvers (that result in minuscule movements in the coach's massive body) until I reach the 180-degree switch. Then I'll have to re-attach the tow dolly and reload the car. Did I mention that it is 9pm, 16 degrees, snowy and icy and dark?

I start by laying down layers of old towels and rags from the door of the coach, up the stairs and across the living room floor to the driver's seat. I'm not about to let road cinders and dirty slushy snow blacken my coach's wall-to-wall carpet in the process. Cat is uncommonly attentive. She's never seen anything like this before.

Next I suit up. I pull on my heavy winter work coat, dawn my wool-lined waterproof work gloves and slide into my sturdy snow boots. Now Cat retreats to the bedroom. She wants no part of whatever is coming next.

Outside I climb under the tow dolly to unhook the safety chains and tire straps that secure the car. Then I back the car off the dolly and park it in safe mode (hazard lights flashing) in the ditch on the opposite side of the road. Next I disconnect the tow dolly from the coach and manu-ally drag it into the ditch in front of the car. One of the passing drivers stops as I'm pulling the dolly across the road, rolls down his window and observes, "Wow, do you have to unhook all of that to turn around?"

"Yes, unfortunately I do." I reply. (Why else would I be doing all this?)

He's encouraging, "It looks like you can fit under it, why don't you try?"

"Well I'll think about that, thank you," I reply without adding, "And what happens when I get stuck and tear off a couple of air conditioners in the process? I'd rather do all this in the cold and in the dark and in the slushy, dirty snow then deal with that!"

He drives away and I continue moving. I climb into the coach's driver seat and turn the wheel all the way to the right in forward gear and press on the gas. The coach inches to the right. I swing the wheel back to the left as far as it goes, put the coach in reverse and press on the gas. The coach's rear wheels roll to the edge of the road. Again, steering wheel all the way to the right, forward. Steering wheel back to the left, reverse. Wheel right, forward. Wheel left, reverse. And two more times both ways until finally I am finally in the middle of the opposite lane in position to reconnect the dolly and load the car.

I've done it. My heart swells with pride. And, despite all the effort that it took, it was quite an effortless feat, far easier than what I had expected. I had executed each step with such precision that I feel like a real motor home mama.

I still don't know how tall the coach is but I guarantee before I hit the road again I will know that number.

# { 23 }

# Stop 3: Pay it Forward

After staying a night at a Gallup motor lodge in which I was over-charged and under-served, I continue down the road to Tempe Diablo Stadium just outside of Phoenix, Arizona.

An hour from my final destination I hear a thumping metallic sound coming from the back end of the coach. It's loud enough to warrant investigation. There could be a problem with the tow dolly, or the car, both of which I can't see from my side mirror. So I start looking for a place pull over to inspect and address whatever is causing the worrisome noise. If I have to call for Road Service then I want to be somewhere safe, and preferably comfortable. Fortunately for me the McDowell Mountain Resort and Casino is just a few miles away.

I pull into the casino parking lot where I encounter no less than 20 automobile brokers and their high-end vintage and collectible vehicles. They are there with their teams of mechanics, preparing the vehicles for the enthusiastic car collectors and buyers attending the annual Barrett-Jackson Auction in Scottsdale this coming weekend. (Barrett-Jackson auctions are recognized as the "World's Greatest Classic Car Auctions".)

I park out of the way of the activities, step out of the coach and to the back of my rig where I discover a mutilated tire rim on the car dolly . . . sans tire. Oh how convenient to be a helpless single woman in times like these. After two or three of the brokers size up my situation and go back about their business one confident, smiling, sexy man trots up to me like a knight in shining armor. He inspects the damage. "Whew, good thing you didn't start on fire!"

Whew, ignorance is bliss. I didn't know that I *could* start on fire.

He's absolutely charming, not even hinting that I am the least bit of an inconvenience to him. Without judgment he suggests that *both* rims and tires should be replaced, and offers his mechanical team's help. "Let's unload your car here and get you over to my spot, out of the way. I'll get my guys to unhook the dolly and remove the tires and rims."

I do as I'm told and practically coast the coach with the damaged dolly over to an ancillary graveled parking area. Here in a man-made clearing bordered by flowering Palo Verde trees and surrounded by the untamed Arizona desert is his semi-private staging lot. Three sparkling new semi-trucks with shiny clean trailers, a couple of decked out pickup trucks, a few sassy sports cars and one Provost motor home line the perimeter of the lot. I feel like I am riding a donkey into a race horse stable.

As soon as I arrive three strapping young men in clean mechanic's coveralls swarm around the car dolly and before I can say, "lickety split" they have those rims removed and placed squarely on pure white mechanic's towels in the trunk of my car. They never let on that they think any differently about my humble get-up than the high-end classic automobiles they are used to handling.

My knight-in-shining-steel-and-wheels hands me his business card with a list of repair parts scribbled on the back.

I zip down to Phoenix in my Saturn and return with the parts, lickety-split. Within minutes, the crew in their spotless coveralls complete the repairs, mount the tires and rims on the dolly and load my car. I am road ready. As I pull away the charming knight flashes me a sexy smile, waves and reminds me, "Pay it forward!"

I surely will. Mechanical troubles in a spot where dozens of mechanics are gathered for only *that* weekend in *that* location? What are the chances?

That's just too good to be true, even for a believer like me. Paying it forward is the least I can do.

# { 24 }

# Drippy Destination

Thanks to my knight-in-shining-steel-and-wheels and his crew I'm back on the road to Tempe, AZ. A quick 50-minute drive and I'm in the heart of the Salt River Valley (aka Valley of the Sun), cruising through mid-afternoon traffic with the finesse and confidence of a stunt car driver on a go-cart track.

My least favorite part of coach life is sometimes the trip between locations. Kind of ironic since I'm living in a house on wheels, but the delays and challenges of the past three days have zapped the fun out of "living the dream".

So many people who hear of my adventure tell me they wish they could do what I'm doing. They admire me and think I have courage. They wish they could do something equally as daring in their own life. I think they give me too much credit. I'm living out the consequences of my decisions, that's all. My priorities powered this adventure, the same propellant rest inside each of them.

My dream has turned into reality, and reality is not always comfortable . . . or fun. In addition to all the challenges I had starting back in

Colorado the troubles didn't end when I arrived at my final destination in Tempe. I know I emptied all the water out of the coach's water lines before I left Coffeyville, Kansas. I remember thinking about how the western winter temperatures could damage the coach's water lines. So imagine my surprise when, after hooking up to my new water source and turning on the kitchen spigot, I see water gushing out from under my kitchen cabinet and feel the spongy wet carpet through my slippered feet!

And that's not all. Next thing I know there is water seeping out from underneath the shower stall. Even the corner of the bedroom, which is on the other side of the bathroom wall, is squishy.

And through the window I hear what sounds like rain water over-flowing from roof line gutters . . . but the water I hear is actually streaming out of my rear wheel wells!

Darn pooey! I have been looking forward to a few days of rest before starting my new assignment. Now I'll be talking to neighbors to trou-bleshoot and then calling a plumber instead.

Turns out I forgot the most important part of draining the water lines: draining the hot water tank that feeds those lines. The Colorado cold turned the water inside the tank into a frozen wedge that cracked the thing wide open. The sunny days melted the ice, and the cold winter nights refroze it. The thawing ice seeped through the water lines loos-ening couplings along the way which caused the water leaks in the bedroom, the bathroom, and down through the wheel wells.

Two hours and one thousand dollars later the water is contained. Cat and I eat a good dinner and fall asleep to the calming sounds of a hoot owl just after dark.

# { 25 }

# Baseball Season at TDS

The Phoenix metro area spreads out across the Salt River Valley like syrup on a pancake. Its five million inhabitants live on the flat landscape in diverse communities, some of which sprouted as suburbs a few decades ago, and others, ancient agricultural settlements that are over two thousand years old.

Tempe, due west of Phoenix, began as one of those ancient agricultural settlements. It was inhabited by the Hohokam people, ancestors of the Pima tribe until the 15th century when they abandoned the area. In the 1800's the area around Tempe became a territorial settlement of the United States. Today it is a thriving college town, home to Arizona State University. And for six weeks every spring the Los Angeles Angels of Anaheim major league baseball team calls Tempe Diablo Stadium (TDS) home.

I am so excited to begin my job at the stadium, and not because I am a baseball fan. I'm excited because I've had the good fortune to attend a few Spring Training baseball games in seasons past and I have to say that there aren't too many better ways to spend an afternoon in March in Arizona. Grab a brat, a beer, and a bag of peanuts and sit back and watch the show.

Baseball fans know that Spring Training Season doesn't start for another four weeks, and so my friends and family are questioning why I'm here so early.

Well, those hot dogs and peanuts don't just magically appear in the stands on Opening Day. In fact, the stands themselves need to be set up, including the food booths, and the team merchandise booths, and the tents, and the soda and beer coolers, the grills, utensils, signage, work areas, cash registers, credit card machines, beer taps – and the electricity and water to run all of it. While most of you are doing your last-minute Christmas shopping, the concessionaires are finalizing contracts, obtaining liquor licenses, completing health department inspections, and screening workcampers for employment. The baseball team is studying last season's plays and our service team is studying last season's sales in preparation for the fired up fans who will attend this season's games.

Basically an entire village is erected, supplied and staffed, after which all facets of game day operations are expertly choreographed in order to keep everyone, from team owners to young fans, captivated and content throughout each and every game. Did you know that last year we sold 35,000 hot dogs during only 15 games? – That's about 1700 hot dogs/hour! And that doesn't include all the rest of the food options -- hamburgers, chicken sandwiches, chips, nachos, Italian ice, hot pretzels, even portobello mushroom sandwiches and pizza. An amazing amount of effort goes into pulling off a successful season and when the entire process happens without the fans noticing we know we've done our jobs well.

It's a lot of work, and a lot of fun. Now, after three weeks of cleaning, inventorying, stocking and training we're finally one week away from opening day.

The excitement builds among our workcamper staff members every day. Workers scramble throughout the stadium to complete their to-do lists in preparation for opening day. The final food and beverage products were received yesterday. Vendor banners have been installed in the concession stands and signage pointing where to find your favorite eats and how much they'll cost you has been posted as well. Maintenance men repaint faded dugout graphics and directional signage, and the lawnmower is in continual motion on the field. The stadium security team reviews crowd control standards, and the Tempe Diablo members (the city's Spring Training Booster Club) review parking lot procedures and rotational post duties.

Individuals working like a colony of ants turn this temporarily erected facility into a close-knit community. Some come to be a part of the history of Tempe Diablo Stadium. Some are long-time Tempe residents proud of their city's role in the great American sport. And some come because they are die-hard California Angels fans thrilled to earn a buck and catch a glimpse of their favorite players while they bag up peanuts and bun up hot dogs. Many return year after year to participate in this spring ritual.

On Opening Day a great sense of accomplishment fills the air when the gates open and fans flood the stands for the first game of the season. Twenty-one games will be played in the month of March. One week after the final game the entire stadium will be returned to its pre-season state: empty and vacant. The season will be history, and I'll be on to my next gig.

# { 26 }

# Pavilion Party

I was hired as the Tempe Diablo Stadium Pavilion Supervisor for the spring season but I joined the staff early to assist with all the other tasks that had to be accomplished in the weeks before opening day. During that time, I helped hire and train employees and distribute equipment and products. I made signs, created reports and tracked inventory. I did pretty much anything I was asked to do and enjoyed every minute of it. And I made sure not to shirk my primary responsibility – the Pavilion. It was ready for all of the premium ticket holders that would fill it to capacity on opening day and every game day thereafter.

Fans that purchase Pavilion tickets enjoy an upgraded game experience. They have full access to an All-You-Can-Eat picnic fare buffet and sit at cloth covered dining tables. They have their own bar just steps away from their seats. There are only a few "bleacher seats" and not the aluminum backless kind that fans fill on the deck below the pavilion. Sturdy white cushioned seats are set up on portable black carpeted risers. They look more like they belong at a wedding where guests will dance to orchestra music rather than something you'd find at a baseball field.

The Pavilion set-up appeals to those looking for a quieter, more relaxed way of watching the game while entertaining clients, or showing appreciation to employees, or simply staying out of the maddening crowds below. They keep a casual eye on the game but mostly they're sipping beers, eating hot dogs, brats, peanuts and popcorn while chatting with others in the Arizona spring sunshine, during this, the best time of the year.

In addition to running the Pavilion operations I also manage services for the discerning guests that rent the stadium's private suites, also located on this upper deck. The suites are where prestigious businessmen relax in leather couches and over-sized lounge chairs and watch the game through windowed walls above and behind home plate. I plan menus and oversee service for city officials, team owners and players' wives, among others. Occasionally a non-ranking guest will rent a suite, like the day that a Tempe family rented one so their Aunt Edith could celebrate her 90th birthday at the ballpark. Watching that family celebrate was one of my favorite days of the season.

There are no permanent food preparation facilities up here, unlike each of the food stands on the main deck. We have a portable makeshift kitchen set up behind heavy white tarps. We work in very primitive conditions with only minimal refrigeration, water supplied by two insulated, super-sized "thermoses" (known as cambros in the catering business), and 2 4'x6' gas grills. As the manager, my tiny-living mentality is critical -- and my greatest strength.

The pavilion is located as far away as possible and on the opposite end of the stadium from all of our resources: equipment, food, beer, (Heaven forbid we should run out of beer!) and everything else we might need. A trip to retrieve any necessity requires plowing one step at a time through the herds of people on the main level to obtain it. It's not like swimming against the tide, it's more like paddle boarding on a rip current. In such cases I am the designated go-fer and the skill of walking great distances triple-time to secure items, which I honed at BuyItOnline.com, is serving me well.

Each day at exactly game start time (on the dot!) all of the hubbub of activity comes to a screeching halt as the announcer invites everyone to stand for the National Anthem. The crowd eagerly responds. Each day I participate. I focus my attention on the brightly colored flag that is mounted high on a pole on the top of the dusty dry rock mountain behind left field. I put my hand on my heart and hear myself sing, "Land of the free and home of the brave". I am so grateful to be free and thankful to practice a tiny bit of bravery in some way every day. I'm grateful for this moment of intentional acknowledgment, and then the game begins. Chaos quickly ensues. It's another day of Spring Training.

# { 27 }

# MVNP

As soon as the last grill of the last hot dog stand at Tempe Diablo Stadium is cleaned and stored for the season I return to my rented RV space to prepare for my departure. I am headed to Colorado for my first gig in a National Park.

I stow utensils, clothes, and toiletries into the coach cabinets, pull in the awning, unhook my utilities and say farewell to my neighbors and Ed, the RV park manager. Some of my neighbors look at Ed and see a crotchety old man, but I see a sad one.

Ed is eighty years old. He closes the office every day during the lunch hour so he can visit his wife of 58 years in the local care facility for Alzheimer's patients. Peering through the office door into the manager's apartment I see remnants of their life together everywhere.

Ed and I get along well. Once my tab is settled he smiles and tells me that he'll have a spot waiting for me any time I want to come back. I'll miss Ed.

By now Cat reads our departure procedure like an itinerary. She is already nestled in her traveling position on the bed pillows at the rear of the coach.

We depart Phoenix without a hint of trouble and very little traffic. It is early morning and I am looking forward to tackling the curves up and out of the valley. Unlike the last time, this time I am relaxed and confident driving up the interstate. I still have some trepidation cruising down the highway into Verde Valley but this time I efficiently downshift, and coast, and engage the brakes like the professional semi-truck drivers alongside me.

The 500 mile trip still takes me two days. The first evening I pull off the road, park, and sleep comfortably in the coach in the high desert plains near the state line. The next day I arrive at Mesa Verde National Park (MVNP) late in the afternoon. The main office for the Park's Concessionaire is located across the road from the Park Entrance on a plot of land known as Point Look Out (PLO).

Back around the 1950's the US Park Service ran a campground with RV and tent sites on the PLO property. It also built a gas station and convenience store there, and cabins to house Park Rangers.

In the 1990's the Park Service upgraded MVNP's facilities by retiring PLO and moving all of the visitor services -- camping sites, convenience store, a lodge, several dining facilities, gift shops, and Park Ranger housing -- into the Park. PLO was abandoned and later sold to the current owner, the Concessionaire.

Two employers staff the park. One is the US government which hires all the Park Service employees: Park Rangers, Road & Building Maintenance Crew members and Law Enforcement Officers. The other employer, the Concessionaire, is the company that hires all the people who cook and serve food and beverages, and check guests in and out of the lodge and the campgrounds. The Concessionaire hired me to manage the lodge's dining room and lounge.

The Concessionaire offers fair wages, free housing and daily meals to all their employees. As a manager, I am given the option to live in my own recreational vehicle in the PLO campground or bunk with another manager in the aforementioned Ranger cabins. Other cabins (bare bones cabins referred to as "WOBs") about the size of tool sheds, have been erected on the PLO tent sites and are reserved for line employees who bunk two to a shed for the season.

Amenities on the property include a community laundry room and bathhouse, and a recreation center comfortably furnished with oversized couches, pool and ping-pong tables, a library of books and movies, computer work stations and a full-sized professional kitchen and dining area. Farther to the back of the property are picnic tables, a bonfire pit and horseshoe spikes. Time off here will be a real life "Throwback Thursday" experience, revisiting summer camp.

I will not be staying in this camp community at PLO. Instead I have chosen to reside in one of the three RV spaces deep within the Park that are contracted to the Concessionaire. I'm looking forward to this semi-isolated camp experience.

The HR Manager warns me that the speed limit maxes out at 45mph through the park and it will take me at least 40 minutes to get to my coveted space. She alerts my new and only neighbors-to-be to be on the lookout for me.

I hop into the coach with a park entrance pass, directions to my space, and information about the manager's training tomorrow morning. I ignore Cat's "Let-me-out" meows, pull out of PLO, cross the overpass and cruise through the park gates just before sunset. I grin at the "Car in Tow Prohibited" sign as I round a bend and glance back to check on my car in tow.

Mesa Verde (Spanish for "green table") is home to some of the best preserved ancestral Puebloan cliff dwellings in the world. Ancestors of current-day Pueblo Indian tribes settled here about 1400 years ago and built stone and stucco communities in the sheltered alcoves of the sandstone canyon walls. They thrived for centuries cultivating and harvesting corn, beans and squash in this semi-arid environment. Then, mysteriously, they abandoned their dwellings and left the area.

The entire park is situated on a geological formation called a "cuesta", a tilted mesa. Mesa Verde's cuesta inclines at a seven degree angle and is intersected by branching canyons carved by wind and water erosion over eons.

The first 10 miles into the Park is a steady winding climb through canyons and around hairpin curves up to the mesa top. It's hard to focus on the road with all the dramatic scenery that surrounds me so I pull into the High Point Scenic Lookout to have a look around.

Here at the very top of the cuesta I can see the slope of the mesa and take in the 360-degree view. I spot the LaPlata Mountains of Colorado, Shiprock Butte of New Mexico, the Blue Mountains of Utah and the Sleeping Ute Mountain on the Ute Mountain Ute Tribe Reservation that flanks the park's western border. Cat stares out from her perch inside the coach window and meows and meows at me as I gaze across the horizon.

I climb back inside and put the coach in gear. I don't want to be setting up in the dark. Five miles beyond the Lookout I pass Far View Lodge where I will manage the restaurant. Then I coast the remaining five miles down the seven degree grade to the end of the road, where my new neighbors-to-be, two well-groomed men, are standing, waiting for me, grinning from ear to ear, exuding contentment.

The tall boyish one with distinguishing gray hair introduces himself, "Hello new neighbor, welcome, I'm David,"

"Hello, aloha, I'm Dennis," the older, wiser man's words roll off his tongue like a late night soul music radio announcer, "Welcome to Shangri la!"

Immediately I fell in love with both of them.

"It's not easy to find your way in, so just follow me. And go slow. The road's kind of rough this time of year," David says and starts walking me down the road as if he were towing me on an invisible leash.

Dennis follows behind the coach, down the rutted dirt road to a cul-de-sac with 3 RV spaces arranged like private lots in a remote vacation setting. On the way David points to a weathered wooden shed where a washer and dryer are located and a minute later he gestures toward the low-hanging Wi-Fi cable along the side of the drive.

I see my spot so intimately flanked by pinion pines that I hope I'll be able to fit in it. I hop out, unload the car, unhitch the car dolly and stop to introduce myself. These two charming men are partners who have been returning to this spot for the past eight years. They came here from Hawaii where they lived together for eight years before that. They call this place magical and judging from the wave of serenity they are both emitting I know I'm going to love it here.

"Climb back in to your rig and we'll guide you into your space," David offers, "And then we'll have wine. He speaks the words slowly and melodically in a Barry White timbre with a Liberace smile. "Do you prefer white or red?" I hop back in to take them up on their first offer in a hurry to get to their second. David directs me via my rear view mirrors and Dennis returns with a full glass of red.

While we chat I tend to my hook-up chores. Our cats share polite little sniffs followed by simultaneous hisses. Once my water, power and sewer are connected Dennis, David and I gather in their aluminum-sided retro remodeled Avion camper.

They give me the low down on what to expect here in this National Park and the etiquette that will keep the park rangers from micro-managing our campground. They map out directions to the best places to watch the sun rise and set from our little "Shangri la" and then they disclose tips about the workplace environment to keep me on my toes through training tomorrow.

Thoroughly entertained and by now a bit tipsy, I step out of their camper into pitch black dark and crispy cold air. I look up. The sky is so studded with stars it looks like a black velvet blanket sprinkled with Swarovski crystals. I have to blink back tears. I'm breathless with overwhelming gratitude.

When I step back into the coach Cat greets me with scolding meows. It's cold AND I have left her alone in the dark. I right my wrongs by turning on the lights and the heat. I don my flannel pjs and plunge under my featherbedding. She pounces on top, nudges my legs into a ninety-degree angle and curls herself into me.

It's so quiet I wonder if I will be able to sleep. But within minutes I relax in the stillness. And then I hear the hoot owl in the branches above my head and doze off.

# { 28 }

# Top of the Cuesta

Of course the first thing about Mesa Verde that caught my attention when I was searching for a summer location was its close proximity to where my sons live. From the Park I head west through the quiet little town of Mancos, Colorado, through the serene Cherry Creek valley, over the treacherous Hesperus Hill, down through the south end of Durango, and then out to my sons' homes in sleepy Bayfield. It's about an hour drive from Mesa Verde, just down the street in relative terms to me.

I'm familiar with this Park. In my 20's, when I first moved to Durango, it was a place to point at and say, "Hmm, someday I'd like to visit there." But I was young and the area outside of the park had so much more to offer a college kid like me. Camping on rugged Lizard Head Pass, soaking in Dutton Hot Springs, tracking bear at McPhee Reservoir and catching a Blue Grass Festival in Telluride all superseded investigating the remains of an ancient civilization in a National Park.

Eventually I made the Park my destination for a weekend and fell in love with it. My friends and I booked rooms at the Far View Lodge atop the cuesta for an unforgettable weekend. We explored the canyons, hiked the trails and climbed ladders in and out of cliff dwelling during the days. In the evening we'd retire to the lodge veranda to sip champagne and watch the sun edge to the horizon. Then we'd teeter downstairs to the dining room to watch the sun waft shadows across the canyon walls from the floor-to-ceiling windows while we dined on wild game delicacies.

Standing in the dining room as the manager now, 30 years later, I feel the awe well up inside me again. I thought that I was seeing the wonders of this land through my starry-eyed innocence back then. But now I know differently. This park is a prestigious World Heritage Site. Tonight and every night people come here from all over the globe to experience this timeless American treasure. I hear diners speaking German, French, Chinese, Japanese, Spanish and Italian. The languages mingle harmoniously with the Native American flute music playing in the background.

I watch guests leave their tables between courses to step out outside and capture photographic images of clouds, shadows, rainbows and never-ending sky. I can't imagine any spot in the world where Mother Nature's dramatic skyscapes are more impressive.

Spectacular sunsets are just the beginning. Watching afternoon thunderstorms travel across the cuesta is like viewing a George Lucas light show with lightning as the star performer instead of fake light sabers. After the storms come dramatic rainbows. First a single rainbow. Then a double. Then unbroken parallel arches in full color. Sights so stunning they defy human imagination.

I feel privileged. But the kids that work under me, ehh, not so much. I call them kids because they mostly resemble the Lost Boys that Peter Pan encountered (both male and female in this case). Some are working their own plan to travel and visit the National Parks while they are young. Some are under-employed college grads unable to fit into the corporate mold who have chosen alternative work and lifestyles instead. And then some are just lost young'uns in the world, looking for the next party and hoping they can outrun responsibilities for as long as possible.

I call them kids but several are my age. One chides me when I inadvertently say the word in front of him, "Kids? If we're kids, then what are you? An embryo?" I laugh. To me "kids" is a term of endearment. I choose to take his humorous remark in the same spirit.

I love these kids just like I love my own. But I don't always like them, if you know what I mean. By the end of each evening I'm tired. I can't wait to close down the restaurant and send the last of the "kids" down the hill on the employee bus to PLO. There they'll engage in their wind-down activities and then retire to their WOBs, (an acronym for "With Out Bathrooms"). They have aptly named their little community "Wobville".

I, on the other hand, pop into my car and take a quick cruise down a hill in the opposite direction. There I stumble from my car to my coach in the dark, trying not to trip on or bump into anything that might wake my neighbors at this midnight hour. Once I'm inside Cat greets me with her usual disdainful meows. I try to placate her as I change from work to bed clothes. (She knows how to make me feel guilty.) Once she's satisfied that she's made her point she cuddles up next to my leg and beds down for the night. The last sound I remember is the hoot owl outside my window as sleep comes over me.

# { 29 }

# Trouble in the Park

Cat is thrilled with the new wilderness location. So many places to explore and so many lizards to catch! She's quite entertaining -- stalking prey, slinking around the agave cactus and piñon trees, and hiding in the tall grasses. She's a wise cat, a true survivor who's well aware of when she can hunt her prey and how to avoid becoming her predator's prey. Her stealth nature serves her well. I can't tell you how many times I've seen danger pass right before her as she held still in her predetermined safe spot.

But sometimes she hides from *me*. And from her hidden location I'm sure she finds great pleasure in watching me look for her and hearing my frustrated calls. That usually happens right before I head out to work. She knows my routines, including my preference to tuck her safe inside the coach when I'm away. That's when she pulls the hiding trick on me. If she outlasts my persistence to search for her then she's free for the day. Most of the time I eventually find her, but not always.

Today is one of those days. I know she's not entirely safe, but I also know that she won't run off. She'll brutalize lizards to her heart's content and then crawl up into the underbelly of the coach and hide out until I get home. That's a satisfying day for her.

I return home early this evening to find her comfortably sprawled out in the cool of the shade underneath the front of the coach. Within minutes of my arrival the Park Ranger truck pulls up to the coach and two uniformed officers get out and approach me. Cat apparently assumes these visitors are benign and remains where she is.

"That your cat?"

"Yes, it is," I smile.

The officer doesn't smile back.

"Well, she needs to be confined, can't be running around the park unleashed," the senior officer chides.

Seeing that I'm not impressed he continues, "Do you have any idea the damage that cats do to the natural environment? How many native species they kill?"

"I understand," I reply, knowing better than to plead my case with law enforcement, "I'll keep a closer eye on her."

He stands in front of me with a this-is-serious pose, his sturdy boots hip distance apart, hands on his hips, chest out and accentuated by the extra bulk of his bullet-proof vest. I wonder if he had to go through extra training to keep a straight face while confronting serious situations like this one.

"I'll give you a warning ticket this time, but next time it'll come with a fine."

What? A warning ticket? Where on earth has she been wandering?

I shuffle her into the coach and start ranting to her in a tone that clearly expresses the seriousness of her offense. She cowers slightly (which is totally uncharacteristic for her – I actually have her attention for once) and plops herself into a napping pillow, curls up and dismisses me.

The next morning I trust her enough to let her stay outside while I take a shower. She obediently shows up when I call her to come in just before I leave for work. She hops in the coach and as I exit and lock the door behind me I notice a pile of sapphire blue feathers on the ground at my feet.

Not only is it becoming apparent that the park ranger knows her better than I do, she confirms it by leaving remnants of a cat-murdered bird in plain sight. I am mortified and I tell her so in no uncertain terms through the coach's open window. I don't care about the ugly little lizards that she kills bite by bite but this is going too far.

The next day as I recount the story to my colleagues, my boss chimes in, "Was that your cat? She was sitting outside of the Spruce Tree Café the other day. I thought it was kind of odd to see a cat in a National Park."

The picture is becoming a little clearer. The Spruce Tree Café isn't far from the coach, and if she is comfortable there I know it won't be long before she wanders over to the Chief Ranger's Office adjacent to it. I will have to keep a closer watch on her. Leashing is out of the question but she understands the word "grounded" as well as my sons had. And just like them she will test me.

Day three passes without incident, and on the morning of day four she obediently, if not reluctantly shuffles into the coach when I call. With no signs of cat-perpetrated killings anywhere and my newly law-abiding pet tucked inside I consider the matter closed.

Day seven -- I call and call but no cat appears. Surely she has learned her lesson. She is probably innocently napping somewhere nearby. Finally, with one last worried look back, I head for work.

When I return late that night Cat doesn't pop out from under the coach to great me, which is unusual. I walk the premises looking for her. I call and call. I search and call some more. I wander around hoping to see her crawl out from under one of the Park vehicles in the area. My expectant calls dim to determined whispers. It's the middle of the night and I don't want to wake my neighbors.

I don't hear her meows. I don't see here anywhere.

Maybe something has scared her up a tree. Maybe she is stuck up a tree. Maybe she is waiting and watching until some danger has passed. This has happened a handful of times in our eight years together. Each time I worried myself sick but all the horrifying scenarios that I imagined never came to pass. So I return to the coach. I tuck myself into bed and turn out the light.

A minute after I settle into the perfect sleeping position I hear a heavy-duty engine approach. The engine cuts off, a truck door slams and heavy boots stomp toward my door. I am terrified. Then a firm knock shakes the coach.

"Just a minute," I yell. I gather my robe and my courage.

"Who is it?" I try to keep my voice from shaking.

"Park Law Enforcement ma'am." I'm surprised to hear the husky voice of a woman.

I'm now confused as well as afraid. I open the door just a crack. I'm blinded by the light beam from her over-sized flashlight.

"How can I help you?"

"Do you know this cat?" the officer asks handing me her flip phone opened to an image of my precious Cat imprisoned in a portable steel kennel.

Fury overrides every other emotion swirling in my body, "Yes, she's mine."

"Found her sitting outside of the Chief Ranger's office this after-noon. All pets in the Park need to be confined ma'am."

"Need to see your driver's license. I'll run it and if we don't find anything then I'll let you know how to get your cat back."

Humph. The only crime here is that a law abiding citizen is being submitted to such an intrusion in the middle of the night. But then I realize that if I was a completely law abiding citizen my cat would be here with me instead of confined to an animal jail cell.

She returns with my license and a ticket attached to her clipboard. "Ok, we're all good. Just need your signature on this and I'll release your cat back into your custody. If she's caught again you may be re-quired to serve jail time."

"Yes, I understand," I submit again, keeping my cool. (Jail time . . . really?)

She hands me my copy of the ticket, retrieves my cat and places her in my arms as she bids me goodnight.

Cat seems untroubled by her capture and imprisonment. As soon as she has all four feet planted on the floor she starts meowing for a saucer of cream. It's her version of my glass of red wine. I pour for both of us, settle back into bed and simultaneously scold and pet her. She humbly accepts both.

The next morning I pay my $100 fine and make arrangements to relocate from my current space into one of the RV spaces at PLO, ad-jacent to "Wobville". There the rules are the same, pets must be confined. But penalties for an inevitable slip up do not include jail time.

# { 30 }

# End of the Season

One of the best things about seasonal employment is the ability to begin the countdown to your last day of work on the first day of the season. It's mid-October in Mesa Verde National Park and the fall foliage has blanketed the park in gold, amber and orange. Bear sightings are frequent in the early mornings and you can hear the elk bugle every night. There are only ten days left on the countdown. This has been an unusually long seasonal position, over 194 days and I'm looking forward to the last of it.

We've already seen the first snow fall and half of the staff have gone to new locations for the winter. My options are still open. I waiver between heading south to Texas to dry-dock on the beaches of Padre Island or do the same in the wide-open desert BLM lands outside of Quartzite, Arizona. Both locations are great winter hot spots that friends I met working at BuyItOnline.com turned me on to.

I'm always welcome back at BuyItOnline.com but modern day gold-rush types encourage me to head to North Dakota to cash in on the booming fracking business there.

"You've got your own housing, that's the most important thing," an encouraging fellow workcamper points out. Well that may be, but it's not the only thing I would need to survive winter in that northern climate.

If I do go north it will be for the sugar beet harvest in North Dakota, Minnesota or Nebraska. What I've heard about the beet harvest intrigues me but I've already missed a good part of the season there.

Year-end will soon be here. My heart is searching for reasons to stay in Colorado so I can be with my sons and their families through the holiday season. Before leaving Tempe Diablo Baseball Stadium seven months ago I committed to work the following season. So it's easy to justify staying in Colorado and heading directly south to the stadium with my start date only ten weeks away.

My ex-husband, Gary, and his wife, Bonnie, recently purchased an old ranch near Bayfield and not far from Mesa Verde. They have invited me to park on their property for as long as I want. They have even gone so far as to offer a real roof over my head, inviting me to make myself at home in their upstairs suite, complete with bedroom and private bath. I've stayed there several times before already and even for an extended stay when I helped them renovate their classic old house.

Bonnie especially dotes on me, calling up the stairs each morning, "Breakfast is ready, how do you want your eggs today?" As I leave the house each day she reports what their plans are, what time dinner will be served and what she'll serve.

It may seem odd that I am so intimately connected to a man I divorced 25 years ago, and to the wife he married over 10 years ago.

Not really so odd though, if you've given any thought to what is promised in nearly every marriage ceremony: "until death do us part". The Good Book says that a marriage connects you to the person you marry for life, regardless of how that plan plays out. Even if you divorce, or move across the country, or halfway around the world from each other, your lives are never separate again. That's doubly true if you share children.

Gary and I had more than our fair share of disagreements in our married and post-divorce years. The change point in our relationship came well after we were divorced when our youngest son graduated from high school.

Gary and Bonnie invited all those travelling to attend the event to stay with them in their home. So my well-mannered father and his German wife came from Maine. My sophisticated mother traveled from Michigan, and my European ex-husband and I came from Arizona. We spent a full weekend together to celebrate the event.

In truly redneck form we gathered in their backyard and dined on homemade Rocky Mountain oysters (prepared in a turkey fryer by our son). We took an afternoon walk through their hay fields, pastures, orchards, and along the river that ran through their hundred-acre spread.

That evening we gathered around the china-dressed dining room table and grinned at each other in amazement. Here we were, exs upon exs, comfortably conversing around a dinner table, laughing, and toasting the future of the two young men who had brought us to this place in time . . .

The conversation lulled. A bashful silence blanketed the table. What started years ago as each diner's decision to treat "the other" with common courtesy and respect had now blossomed into a gathering filled with love and acceptance.

From that evening on my relationship with my ex, Gary, and his wife, Bonnie, has flourished. Year after year we share precise time together with our children, and precious time together building the relationship between us.

So, it's really not so odd that I should reside in their backyard. I think I'll rest there while I reflect on my first year of living on the road. I know I won't hear any objections from Cat.

# { 31 }

# Q's & A's

## Do you still like your dream home?

I couldn't be happier. I'm really enjoying the simplicity of living in the coach. Everything you need and nothing you don't.

I can sit on my living room couch and reach books and a beverage on my kitchen table without taking a step. My kitchen counter doubles as an end table for the living room, no dusting required.

I can clean the entire coach, front to back, including the bathroom, kitchen and cleaning the floors in less than 40 minutes. That sure beats an entire day of house cleaning.

The coach is my adventure vehicle and my safe haven. I doubt that I will ever tire of it.

## What are you cooking and eating?

When I first started out I was as intimidated by operating the coach's stove as I was about every other portion of the coach, so I shied away from cooking as long as I could. I was satisfied with fresh veggies, cheese and crackers, peanut butter and jelly sandwiches, and re-hydrated meals-in-a-cup. But eventually I craved my own cooking enough that I mustered the courage to light the pilot light and give my stove a try. As is the case with most every coach experience I have had, it was much easier to do than expected, and not worth all the turmoil I put myself through in the process of avoiding the task at hand. (Oh if I could just dive into things instead of entertaining my fantastical fears first!)

At any rate I've found cooking in the coach to be a delightful experience. It's like camping with all the luxuries. A tiny kitchen has its drawbacks if you're cooking for a family. But cooking for one is actually quite easy in this confined space.

The refrigerator is perfectly sized to fit a week's worth of essentials, just enough space so everything gets used before it makes its way to the back of the unit and spoils. There's plenty of storage space for non-perishables and I've transferred all of my staples from boxes and plastic bags to glass storage containers so that unwanted critters are not enticed to creep or crawl their way into my cabinets. This see-through storage system makes it easy to pull out and/or inventory my ingredients. And it adds a touch of class to my picnic-style pantry.

I brought my favorite utensils with me: copper pots and pans, a cast iron skillet and stew pot, and a few good knives. I have a three burner stove (which is one more than I typically use on a regular basis when cooking in my more traditional suburban Phoenix home), a microwave (which is much more efficient than the one I had in my suburban home), and an oven (which is so small that the heating element sits one inch below the baking rack, which is one inch from the ceiling of the oven's interior). The oven is the only thing in the entire coach that is completely useless.

Small spaces appear even smaller when covered with clutter so I keep up with the clean up as I go. Cleaning up after eating usually takes five minutes or less. (I know, I've timed it!)

I have paper plates and disposable cups but prefer to use my sterling silver flatware and china as much as possible, even if I'm just cooking up a quick batch of oatmeal in the morning. Doing so brings an element of civility to what could otherwise be a pretty primitive eating experience.

And I try to keep fresh flowers on the dining table at all times. You'd be surprised how much elegance even a simple bouquet can add to the dining experience. It brightens the entire coach.

## Are you still taking Navy showers?

I am delighted to say "Negatory" to that. Once I was past the coldest winter days I decided to test the waters (literally)! I allowed the shower to run for as long as it took to comfortably wash my body from head to toe. I emerged from the shower, scrubbed from head to toe, fully satisfied, and with hot water to spare. From that day forward I have enjoyed leisurely showers.

I'm also more relaxed about using my propane, water and electricity. That's not to say that I ignore the carbon footprint I and my coach leave behind. I consciously conserve all of my resources however and whenever I can.

## What about laundry?

I have to admit that doing my laundry at a laundromat is not my favorite way to clean my clothes or spend time. But most RV parks have washers and dryers on the property just for their residents. This keeps me out of commercial, general public laundromats, and so far I've been quite comfortable with the arrangement. Usually there's one or two other RVers doing their laundry at the same time so it's a great place to make new workcamper friends.

I could install a washer/dryer specifically designed for RV's in the coach but I would have to forfeit my shower stall for this convenience. I'll never trade my civilian showers for clean clothes!

# Is Cat still content with the coach life?

Not only is Cat loving the gypsy life, she comes up with new ways of telling me so all the time. We've learned to communicate via voice inflections and not-so-subtle behavioral clues.

Her scratch pad is stationed directly in front of the bedroom heating vent. Most of the time she beelines through the coach for this destination after going outside on cold days. It's her version of "sitting by a fire".

On other days she makes a beeline for the dashboard to monitor passing dangers, or watch the evening wildlife activities, both animal and human. She's safe and secure up there, like a queen in a Pope-mobile.

Outside she's learned how to use the coach's door hook as an emergency signal for me to open the door and let her in NOW. With one swipe of her paw the hook lifts up and snaps against the side of the coach. I'm impressed with her ingenuity.

For the most part she stays fairly close to the coach and the safe harbors that are plentiful in its underbelly.

We both enjoy our leash-less walks together. She stays within a 30 foot radius of me as we wander through the RV Parks and campgrounds that are our "ever-changing neighborhoods".

Cat revels in the newness of each location. I love to watch her explore her surroundings. She reminds me how wonderful the world is when one is curious.

# Does she mind the movement of the RV while you are on the road?

Oh she's fine on the road. As I've mentioned, she begins each trip nestled deep into the bed pillow in the back of the coach. About an hour into the trip she'll make her way up to the dashboard, take in the scenery and snooze for a while, then disappear somewhere behind my driving seat.

The only time I see or hear from her is when I stop the vehicle. She reappears, usually from the bedroom and meows, letting me know I've just interrupted her nap. Then she crunches on a few pieces of food, sips her water, wanders back to the bed, and takes a long cat leap into her oversize feather pillow. I'd be doing the same if I were in her paws.

# ABOUT THE AUTHOR

Alexis continues to live a gypsy life.
She travels to wherever she is welcomed to speak about the simple
strategies that make day dreams come true.

CPSIA information can be obtained
at www.ICGtesting.com
Printed in the USA
FSOW01n1512150117
29653FS